ALLEN COUNTY PUBLIC LIBRARY

FORT WAYNE, INDIANA 46802

You may return this book to any agency, branch,
or bookmobile of the Allen County Public Library.

WARRIORS AND ADVENTURERS

by
Irene M. Franck
and
David M. Brownstone

A Volume in the Work Throughout History
Series

Facts On File Publications
New York, New York • Oxford, England

WARRIORS AND ADVENTURERS

Library of Congress Cataloging-in-Publication Data

Franck, Irene M.
  Warriors and adventurers.

  (Work throughout history)
  Bibliography: p.
  Includes index.
  Summary: Explores the role throughout history of
warriors, soldiers, adventurers, and outlaws of society.
    1. Military art and science—Juvenile literature.
2. Adventure and adventurers—Juvenile literature.
[1. Military art and science—History. 2. Adventure and
adventurers—History] I. Brownstone, David M.
II. Title. III. Series.
U106.F73   1988   355'.009   87-19947
ISBN 0-8160-1452-3

Printed in the United States of America

10 9 8 7 6 5 4 3 2 1

Contents

Preface

Warriors and Adventurers is a book in the multi-volume series, *Work Throughout History*. Work shapes the lives of all human beings; yet surprisingly little has been written about the history of the many fascinating and diverse types of occupations men and women pursue. The books in the *Work Throughout History* series explore humanity's most interesting, important, and influential occupations. They explain how and why these occupations came into being in the major cultures of the world, how they evolved over the centuries, especially with changing technology, and how society's view of each occupation has changed. Throughout we focus on what it was like to do a particular kind of work—for example, to be a farmer, glassblower, midwife, banker, building contractor, actor, astrologer, or weaver—in centuries past and right up to today.

Because many occupations have been closely related to one another, we have included at the end of each article references to other overlapping occupations. In preparing this series, we have drawn on a wide range of general works on social, economic, and occupational history, including many on everyday life throughout history. We consulted far too many wide-ranging works to list them all here; but at the end of each volume is a list of suggestions for further reading, should readers want to learn more about any of the occupations included in the volume.

Many researchers and writers worked on the preparation of this series. For *Warriors and Adventurers*, the primary researcher-writer was William Laird Siegel; Douglass L. Brownstone and David G. Merrill also worked on substantial parts of this work. Our thanks go to them for their fine work; to our expert typists, Shirley Fenn, Nancy Fishelberg, and Mary Racette; to our most helpful editors at Facts On File, first Kate Kelly and then James Warren, and their assistant Claire Johnston; to our excellent developmental editor, Vicki Tyler; and to our publisher, Edward Knappman, who first suggested the *Work Throughout History* series and has given us gracious support during the long years of its preparation.

We also express our special appreciation to the many librarians whose help has been indispensable in completing this work, especially to the incomparable staff of the Chappaqua Library—director Mark Hasskarl and former director Doris Lowenfels; the reference staff, including Mary Platt, Paula Peyraud, Terry Cullen, Martha Alcott, Carolyn Jones, and formerly Helen Barolini, Karen Baker, and Linda Goldstein; Jane McKean and Marcia Van Fleet and the whole circulation staff—and the many other librarians who, through the Interlibrary Loan network, have provided us with the research tools so vital to our work.

Irene M. Franck
David M. Brownstone

Introduction

Some people work largely outside the normal patterns of everyday society. Though their work may be very highly organized and structured, these outsiders follow different rules than most other people do. Sometimes society approves of their work, even though it involves acts forbidden to most other people, such as a *soldier* killing another human being. Sometimes society disapproves of their work or even considers it beyond the law. Even so, as in the case of *robbers*, people in the society occasionally employ them or turn a blind eye to their activities. The work of these outsiders is often very dangerous. They may be subject to sudden death or imprisonment, and their working life is generally short. On the other hand, because they are not bound by many of the normal restrictions and responsibilities of society, they are sometimes seen—rightly or wrongly—as living a free and even glamorous life. The occupations held by these outsiders we have grouped in this book as *Warriors and Adventurers*.

Warfare began long ago, in prehistoric times, when human beings still lived as hunters and gatherers. But for many thousands of years the general population—men and sometimes women as well—gathered together to form an army whenever it was needed. Professional *soldiers* in organized armies did not appear until later, however, with the rise of the great states of the Middle East, several thousand years B.C. From that time to this, people have relied to a large extent on organized armies to defend their society—and sometimes to attack neighboring countries.

The core of these armies has been the professional soldier. Volunteers and conscripts fill out the army in times of war, then return to their peacetime jobs. Despite the obvious danger of being killed or maimed, some people have always chosen to become soldiers—some for patriotic reasons, some because they have no other employment readily open to them, some because it gave them a chance to see the wider world and participate in great events.

The soldier's counterpart on the sea is the *sailor*. But sailors have traditionally been far more than warriors. They not only fought in battles, but they also handled the ships, acted as *traders*, and were sometimes *fishers* or *whalers*, as well. A ship's discipline is harsh, but sailors do indeed "see the world." In earlier centuries, especially, when many people traveled no more than a few miles from their homes during their whole lifetimes, the sea exerted a powerful attraction. Outside of formal navies, sailors have often also been able to pick and choose which ships to sign on with, a kind of choice open to few people in other occupations. So, however hard the work, the sea has traditionally been seen as offering a free life. As a result, many a young man—and, more recently, young woman—has chosen the life of a sailor.

In the last century, flight exercised a similar fascination, as human beings finally took to the air. *Flyers*, like soldiers, have often fought as warriors in battle. But, like sailors, they have had other jobs as well. Today they fly people and cargo in a network that links countries all over the world. Despite its dangers, flying is one of the most sought-after jobs in the world.

Another job that combines great danger with popular fascination is that of the *spy*. Spies are professionals who seek out information on their enemies to aid their friends. Though some spies have become heroes or martyrs, most—the best—are totally unknown, so successfully do they mask their true work under cover of another activity. Because of this, though spies are popular in fiction, they often make people feel uneasy in real life.

Adventurers of a different sort are *gamblers* and *gamesters*. The practice of betting on the outcome of certain events has roots far back in history. So does the establishment of games for the purpose of betting. While many people are attracted by the possibility of easy winnings through gambling, the professionals are the only ones who win in the long run. Many of them do not bet themselves, but only operate betting games for others. They often do so on the edge of the law. Though gambling is legal in some places, much gambling takes place illegally, beyond the restrictions and control of government. Gamblers and gamesters, therefore, often have rather shady reputations.

Totally beyond the law are *robbers* and other *criminals*. The roots of robbery go back to prehistoric times. From the time people first began to think of things as "private property," there existed robbers to steal them. Some have pursued their trade through outright theft; others have swindled and cheated to gain things that were not rightly theirs. Much human ingenuity has gone into figuring out how to rob others of their rightful property. Beyond that, a smaller number of people have acted as professional *murderers*, hiring themselves out to kill other people.

Robbers and other criminals do not simply act as individuals, however. In many parts of the world in history, they have formed themselves into highly structured organizations, the better to pursue their ends. Sometimes these organizations have risen out of a sense of injustice and self-defense. So it is that some robbers, such as Robin Hood and his merry men or Jesse James and his gang, have become folk heroes, despite the fact that they were outlaws. But even when injustice gave rise to such organizations, the criminal life tends toward violent ends and poses great dangers to society.

Whatever the dangers involved in the lives of these warriors and adventurers, people have often been fascinated by their work—even if they did not themselves wish to join it.

Flyers

Human fascination with flight probably dates back to the primitive desire to soar like the birds. Accounts of people being turned into birds or riding through the sky on such winged creatures as Pegasus abound in myths that span thousands of years. When did people first take to the air? Some records indicate that over 2,000 years ago in China, kites were used to fly observers. And during the Renaissance, scientists such as Leonardo da Vinci designed a variety of devices that could be flown.

However, the distance between theory and reality could be measured in centuries. *Designers* and *scientists* continued to create plans for flying machines that they hoped would enable humans to leave the ground, but these designs were generally of the *ornithopter* variety—machines that copied the actual flight of birds. Finally, developments in chemistry contributed to the

1

By the mid-19th century, hot-air balloons had given rise to visions of skies crowded with passenger flights. ("Air-um Scare-um Travelling" by George Cruikshank, 1843)

search for a flying machine. In the mid-18th century, scientists such as Henry Cavendish and Joseph Priestley successfully isolated lighter-than-air gases.

Joseph Montgolfier of France created a *hot-air balloon*, and other designers used the lighter-than-air gases, such as hydrogen, to fill their balloons. Throughout the rest of the 18th century and all of the 19th century, designers worked to perfect the balloon. The first balloon to carry passengers was launched by Montgolfier in 1782, carrying a sheep, a chicken, and a duck. A month later, an even larger balloon carried two people aloft.

The basis for future flying occupations was established at this time. First, there were the designers of the machines, and second, there were the people who flew them. The primary use of balloons was as a military tool. Balloons could be used as platforms for *observers*, giving a bird's-eye view of enemy formations and troop dispositions. The more ambitious thought balloons could be used to ferry troops and mount assaults on enemy positions. However, balloons were subject to the vagaries of the wind. It was virtually impossible to control a free balloon. Therefore, the major practical use of balloons remained as tethered observation platforms—although many adventurous spirits used balloons to cross mountains and bodies of water.

Experiments with other types of vessels continued. One type of craft which was an outgrowth of balloons was the *dirigible*, usually a rigid, lighter-than-air ship. The most famous designer and builder of this type of craft was the German Count Ferdinand von Zeppelin. Zeppelin toiled for many years at the beginning of the 20th century to create an airship. Many structural difficulties had to be overcome. For example, Zeppelin's first airship, launched in 1900, was 420 feet long. It flew for 18 minutes and buckled in a number of places. However, dirigibles were gradually perfected and by 1909 Zeppelin had sold a number to a private air company.

Dirigibles and other lighter-than-air craft, such as *blimps*, continued to be developed for the next several decades. But deadly crashes, like that of the Hindenburg in 1937, ended public interest in flying these ships. While the experimentation with lighter-than-air craft was interesting, heavier-than-air craft gradually became the leaders of the 20th century. Technology had finally caught up with the age-old aspiration of soaring with the birds.

The close of the 19th century saw the proposal of many designs for flying ships. Before actual flights were tried, many theoreticians researched the subject and published their works. These works formed a backbone for developing practical machines. It is a mistake to believe that

Wilbur and Orville Wright, *bicycle-makers* from Dayton, Ohio, emerged with a complete *airplane* one day. They had read accounts of a German *glider* maker and *pilot*, Otto Lilienthal, who had made thousands of flights in gliders (engineless craft, released from a height) before he was killed testing one. The Wrights were also aware of many other experimenters in the aviation field.

However, in the dawning years of the 20th century, the Wright brothers were the leading heavier-than-air craft designers and builders. Starting with gliders, they improved their designs until at last they were ready to add an engine and attempt powered flight. In 1903, they flew *Flyer*, a *biplane*, several times. Their longest flight lasted over a minute but covered less than 1,000 feet. Over the next five years, the Wrights continually improved their creation. In 1908, Wilber Wright gave a demonstration of their latest plane and stunned the observers. *Flyer III* performed many complicated maneuvers in the air and covered a distance of 80 miles, remaining airborne for three hours. One impressed witness said: "Wilbur Wright is in possession of a power which controls the fate of nations."

After this success, work on such aircraft literally took off. Just 10 years after the original Wright brothers' flight at Kitty Hawk, a few very sophisticated aircraft were capable of flying long distances at speeds of more than 125 miles per hour. This was not without substantial dangers. For example, Orville Wright was severely injured and his passenger killed when their plane crashed in 1908. Many other experimenters lost their lives in the initial conquest of the skies.

Uses for airplanes were debated, and most of the uses considered were military applications. Most of the military adopted a conservative wait-and-see attitude.

The first military use of the airplane was in 1911, when the Italians declared war on Turkey. A few Italian planes flew over Turkish positions and the pilots lobbed some hand grenades at the Turks. The Turks protested this bitterly, claiming that the Italians had hit a hospital. The international community bickered about the use of

planes—bombing from balloons had been prohibited, but second thoughts about airplanes prevented a similar ban on them. At any rate, like most such agreements, they were conveniently ignored during wartime anyway.

During World War I, the evolution of the airplane was fast and furious; the crafts were improved and strategies for their use were developed. *Air Warfare* is an example of an entire new branch of the armed services developing because of a new invention. At the start of World War I, airplanes, used in addition to Zeppelins, were limited to reconnaissance missions, to spy on enemy positions. Each side then produced *fighter planes* to prevent this. Planes were mounted with machine guns to shoot down other planes; this was necessary because ground defenses were not effective in shooting down aircraft. By the end of the war, the performance of the planes had been improved and they had sophisticated armament. A wide variety of

Early airplanes were light, open affairs; here Orville Wright takes his sister Katherine for a ride. (Library of Congress, c. 1915)

types of planes was created. Some were used as fighters and reconnaissance craft, but there were also *bombers*, which could attack targets on the ground.

New military occupations included the people who had to fly the plane—the pilots—as well as *navigators, bombardiers*, and other support people, such as *mechanics* and ground-control staff. Scientists were faced with a new range of problems to overcome. For example, how did the navigator find the target? And once the target was discovered, how did he hit it with a load of bombs? Electronics, radio, and sensitive bombsights were all used to solve these problems.

Then there was the other side of air warfare—how to defend against this unprecedented threat from the sky. Special guns and shells were developed to blast aircraft out of the skies. Barrage balloons were sent aloft to entangle attacking planes. However, it was soon discovered that the most effective antiaircraft weapon was another aircraft. Pilots were trained in the specialized methods of downing opposing planes.

World War I saw the first duel for control of the skies. The Germans in their Fokkers had the advantage over the British and French in the early part of the war. Compared to the soul-grinding misery of the trench warfare beneath, the opposing fighter groups were likened to knights fighting in single combat. In reality, it was not terribly glamorous. The British and French flying in inferior planes were overwhelmed by the Germans. This was later reversed as the Allies obtained better craft. The fighting in the air was just as grueling as the fighting raging on the ground. One British ace fought 23 battles in 14 days before receiving a well-deserved rest.

Flying at this time also was a physically taxing chore. Pilots flew in rather flimsy craft with open cockpits. Weather was a major factor, as was maintenance. Some pilots dove away from their enemy and found their plane was falling apart. Design defects were not uncommon either. It was discovered, for example, that some of the Fokkers' wings disintegrated in steep dives. None of this is surprising, since the designers could hardly have imagined every test their planes would encounter in combat. And it must be remembered that the first successful flight was still just a little more than a decade old.

Perhaps that is why the pilots were idolized. They were obviously risking their lives in something totally new and wonderful. This fascination with pilots and planes remained even after the war, when perhaps the greatest American hero of the time was a pilot—Charles Lindbergh. During the 1920s air travel was in its infancy and the occupations surrounding the airplane were limited to experimentation, design, and piloting. Everyone understood that the airplane was a terrific idea, but no one was quite sure what to do with it. Its military importance had been proven, but what was it good for in civilian life?

The answer came from young pilots like Lindbergh. They pushed the airplane to its limits and proved that commercial flight had a bright future. Lindbergh's flight from New York to Paris was not the first Atlantic crossing. Many pilots of heavier-than-air craft had accomplished that feat. But Lindbergh was the first to do it solo. It took him over 33 1/2 hours of non-stop flying, but he reached his destination, won a $25,000 prize, and captured the imagination of people around the world.

These were golden years for flying. Piloting a plane was a terrific escape and a wonderful adventure. Pilots like Wiley Post and Amelia Earhart were idolized. *Barnstorming* (doing stunt-flying exhibitions), flying the mail, crop dusting, flying cargo and passengers, all held a special thrill. There were records galore to break—distance, altitude, speed. Virtually every year, a new advance was made that extended the airplane's capabilities.

During the 1920s and 1930s, the military also envisioned a rosy future for the plane. In 1921, an Italian flyer, Giulio Douhet, published a book called *Command of the Air*. In it, he claimed that air forces by themselves could win wars by bombing the enemy into submission. Many military strategists believed him. In the 1920s, many theorists believed that bombing could kill more than 50,000 people a week. When World War II came, bombing was indeed terrible, even if it generally was not the cataclysmic happening predicted—except in cities such as Cologne, Dresden, and Tokyo with conventional bombing and Nagasaki and Hiroshima with nuclear bombing.

There was a quantum leap from the aircraft of World War I to those of World War II. In World War I, the aircraft rarely exceeded 100 mph. By the end of World War II, propeller-driven planes were flying faster than 500 mph. Pilots learned new skills in aviation, dogfighting, night flying, and bombing. The technologists were also kept busy. World War II witnessed a dizzying variety of new weapons of offense and defense for air warfare. The British developed radar, and the Germans countered with buzz bombs and guided missiles. Air power soon became a major instrument. The German Luftwaffe swept over continental Europe and greatly aided the German *Blitzkrieg* ("lightning war"). However, it met its match in the British Royal Air Force.

The Battle of Britain gave the new air force supporting the plane a chance to shine. The few professional *flyers* in the British air force—their numbers could be measured in the hundreds—blunted the German air attack and prevented the Germans from achieving air superiority. This, in turn, halted any German plans to invade the British Isles, since they could not possibly have succeeded without total air superiority. Instead they invaded Russia and lost all chances of bringing all Europe under Axis control. The Germans bombed British cities and the British responded in kind. In 1943, many British believed they could end the war with their strategic bomber force alone—and they came relatively close. Flying at night, British bombers devastated many German cities. However, they were unable to crack German morale. American bombers soon joined them and began bombing German cities by day. Yet neither force could reach the heart of Germany, until escorting fighters were developed which could accompany the bombers throughout the missions.

Bomber crews, with the possible exception of submarine crews, had the toughest jobs in the war. Flying in bombers over enemy territory and being subjected to antiaircraft fire and swift enemy fighters was a terrifying business. Most Allied crews had to fly 30 missions. Up to two-thirds of some bomber groups were lost through death, injury, or capture. At some times during 1943 and 1944, flyers were more likely to be lost in action than to survive.

The bombings of World War II gave humanity a good look at modern, total war. Suddenly there were no front lines. When air forces of both sides began to indiscriminately bomb cities, all civilians were marked as combatants. Civilians suffered horribly during this war, more so than during any other war in history.

Air power was also a counter to powerful surface fleets for the first time in World War II. The Japanese had great success with bombers at Pearl Harbor. In the war for the Pacific, the *aircraft carrier* was key. The Japanese were struck a fatal blow by the Americans at the Battle of Midway when they lost most of their carrier force. From that point on, the Americans got stronger while the Japanese declined.

The end of World War II pointed the way of military and commercial flying for the future. The Germans and British had simultaneously developed *jet aircraft* at the end of the war. This new technology formed the foundation for today's *supersonic* craft, which fly faster than the speed of sound. The Germans developed the V1, a type of primitive cruise missile, which could be guided to its target, and the V2, a true *ballistic missile*, which has a free-fall descent from its launch trajectory. These were the foundations for American and Soviet spacecraft and intercontinental ballistic missiles, which form the nuclear arsenals of the superpowers today. The nuclear tip for the German-inspired missiles was developed by the Allies. The nuclear destruction threatened from the air has added a new dimension to war—and indeed, to survival in the world today.

Throughout the 1950s and 1960s *test pilots* began assessing aircraft, pushing them to their limits to find their strengths and weaknesses. Once the sound barrier was broken, aircraft companies built planes that would go increasingly faster and higher. In the commercial field, air travel has become a major industry. And thanks to the jet, commerce and communications have become truly international.

On commercial planes today, pilots and *co-pilots* handle the navigational and flying duties, with the pilot equivalent to the *captain* of a ship, having that title as well. Many pilots have received their initial flight training in the armed services. World War II produced the first major crop of commercial flyers, but many gained their basic experience in the Korean or Vietnam wars, or in peacetime service. Female pilots have flown in the skies for many years. These have included individual pioneers

Modern airplane pilots refine their skills in flight simulators. (By Bill Osmun, from Air Transport Association)

such as Amelia Earhart, as well as special flying groups during World War II. Few women have become commercial pilots, however, except for very small airlines, a pattern that is changing only slowly.

Assisting the pilots on board the plane are a staff of *flight attendants.* Formerly called *stewardesses* and *stewards,* these crew members' most important responsibility is to see to the safety of the passengers in flight, and especially in case of an accident. But as commercial airlines prefer to minimize the danger and to stress the comforts in their competition for passengers, much of the flight attendants' actual duties are involved in dealing with creature comforts, supplying food and drinks, pillows and blankets; making arrangements for music and movies for the passengers who want them; and generally keeping order. They are also widely regarded as "window dressing," their deportment and appearance being a large part of their job qualifications, in the eyes of the airlines. Some stewardesses in years past even had to

Flight attendants take very seriously their responsibility for passenger safety. (By Bill Osmun, from Air Transport Association)

sue in court for the right to keep their jobs after they were married and over 35 years old. Flight attendants are generally trained in special schools, often affiliated with the airlines themselves.

On the ground the air industry also includes many support occupations. Perhaps most vital of these are *air traffic controllers*, who monitor and route planes in flight and especially during landing and takeoff, to avoid collisions. These men and women are highly paid technicians in a high-pressure job, often trained in the armed services. *Aircraft mechanics* apply their special skills to maintain and repair the planes, checking and readying them for each flight. *Ticket agents*, meanwhile, handle all the paperwork involved in reservations and boarding passes, a particularly difficult job when flights have been delayed and many passengers must be rerouted or placed on different flights.

It is hard to believe that air flight is less than a century old. Planes now fly at well over 2,000 mph and can travel thousands of miles without stopping. This is a far cry from the Wrights' flight of a few hundred feet at little more than 20 mph. By the time planes have become a century old, their marvels will have increased again.

Indeed the weapons of destruction spawned by World War II yielded a different kind of marvel: the *rocket*. Thanks to the V2, humans have been able to escape the

Supporting the more glamorous flyers are great numbers of ground personnel, like these ticket agents. (Air Line Employees Association, International)

confines of the Earth. Americans and Soviet pilots became *astronauts* and *cosmonauts*, explorers of space. Space-age occupations from *engineers* to *astronomers* opened up. Unmanned spacecraft have visited several planets, including Mars, Venus, Jupiter, and Saturn; manned craft have landed on the Moon; and reusable shuttle spacecraft have been developed. The dangers involved in these explorations of space were made clear by the tragic accident that killed the astronauts flying the space shuttle *Challenger* in early 1986. But the attractions of space exploration and of flight altogether are so strong that there is no shortage of flyers or astronauts to take up new challenges in the field.

For related occupations in this volume, *Warriors and Adventurers*, see the following:
Sailors
Soldiers
Spies

For related occupations in other volumes of the series, see the following:
in *Scientists and Technologists*:
Astronomers
Chemists
Computer Scientists
Engineers
Geologists
Physicists
in *Manufacturers and Miners*:
Mechanics and Repairers

Gamblers and Gamesters

Gamblers are people who place bets on contests and then trust their luck to win something for nothing. Sometimes they use very sophisticated means of attempting to "beat the odds" which, from the beginning of time, have been stacked against them. *Gamesters* are those who either own or operate gaming houses and casinos, or who are players of games like chess, billiards, and cards. Professional game players are compensated either by gambling directly on their own abilities and luck, or by winning a prize offered to the winner of the game.

Bookmakers or *odds makers*—often called simply *bookies*—are engaged in either the legal or the illegal arranging of bets in such a way that either side of a contest has an equal chance of returning winning money to the bettors. If, for instance, the Harvard football team plays against the Yale team, which happens to be much weaker in that given year, a bookmaker may arrange a 10-point "spread" for that particular game. That means Harvard must not only win, but must do so by more than 10 points in order to beat the spread. If Harvard wins, but by only nine points, then those bettors who placed their money on Yale come up winners. Using this and other systems of equalizing contestants, bookmakers attract more betting on each side, and therefore increase their own chances of winning more money than they lose. While bettors often become professional gamblers, it is the odds makers who usually fill the ranks of this occupation.

Many small-time gamblers win money from time to time, but this hardly makes them professionals. Professional gamblers are those who earn enough money in this way to support themselves financially. The line is thinly drawn, however, because many bettors devote most of their lives to beating the odds and do, in fact, win just enough to get by. Many bookmakers, on the other hand, spend very little time in the "games," but nonetheless earn a fortune. This is particularly true of *mobsters* who make book on games, or bet on the games themselves, as only a small part of their larger operation, which may also include countless other illegal activities that contribute to their incomes.

Gamblers have been known since ancient times in Mesopotamia, Egypt, China, Greece, Rome, and virtually everywhere at every time in human history. But until modern times, the few professional gamblers generally operated as outlaws or infidels. The Romans were ardent amateur gamblers, but professionals were ridiculed and could be sued for monies lost to them by unfortunate bettors. The ancient Hebrews also rebuked professional gamblers. Their illegal gains, if won from a Jew, had to be paid back double; if won from a Gentile, there was no need for them to be repaid, but the gambler was punished nonetheless. Many fundamentalist Moslem nations have held gambling to be illegal ever since the earliest days of the dissemination of their holy book, the Koran, which forbade gambling in any form.

Gambling is an international activity; these are Chinese dice-players near Amoy. (From The New America and the Far East, *by G. Waldo Browne, 1901)*

Although gambling was not a common profession before modern times, many people at least tried their hands at it. Chess, one of the oldest games in the world, was played by the ancient Egyptians, Chinese, Greeks, Romans, and Arabs. Some form of similar board game has existed as long as the recorded history of humankind, perhaps as early as 6,000 years ago when it was played in Mesopotamia. It is not clear whether or not the ancient form of this game involved prizes or bets. In the ruins of ancient Pompeii, loaded dice and gaming tables were found, and Romans openly placed bets on chariot races and gladiatorial duels. Card playing, which is believed to have begun in China in the 12th century A.D., was a major pastime in 16th-century France. During the reign of Henry IV, Paris was the world's card-playing center and "academies of joy"—public gaming houses, what we would now call *casinos*—thrived. In the 17th century, Cardinal Mazarin sought to build the reserves of the French royal treasury by encouraging the building of *hoca* casinos. Hoca was the forerunner of modern roulette, which came into being in the 18th century and was played enthusiastically by the French and Russians, among others.

Undoubtedly gamblers found quick fortunes at the expense of the hordes of bettors who attended ancient horse and chariot races, particularly in Rome. Although such activities were largely illegal, and therefore poorly recorded, we know that these races regularly featured arguments between bettors. An elaborate system was even employed to quickly relay race results back to the crowd via trained pigeons. Roman emperors played dice for large sums of money, but so did common people. Complaints about cheating and lying surrounded these events, so someone was certainly making money, but it is not certain if the winners were professional gamblers.

In the Middle Ages the most prominent professional gamblers were *house owners*, who ran gaming houses in large urban areas like Paris and Amsterdam. They made their fortunes at the expense of the small bettor. There were professional bettors, too, who tried to "break the house"; but few had good fortune, and their careers often ended in a duel to settle their debts. In the 16th century an Italian gamester named Pimentello began making loans to bettors in Paris. Interest rates on repayment were extreme, and he made a fortune on others' misfortunes in an early form of *loan sharking*.

Bookmakers first became professionals toward the end of the 17th century. Their function was derived from that of the former official *intermediate* or "keeper of the match book" in medieval match races between two horses. As more horses entered the races, and thus more bettors entered "the action," the job of the intermediate was split into two separate occupations. The function of judging winning horses was maintained by the intermediate, but that of recording bets and determining who owed what to whom following the race became the function of a new official called the *bookmaker*.

Bookmakers soon gained a reputation for leaving town

Many poor workers gambled away their meager earnings at cards in places like this one. (By Gustave Doré, from London: A Pilgrimage, *1872)*

quickly rather than paying out large sums to bettors who had bought large shares in the favored horse. The more honest ones would "lay off" or "hedge"—that is, transfer to others or rebet—unpromising bets. By the late 19th century, though, bookmakers became more secure in and even assured of their profits by using a new wager technique called *pari-mutuel*. By this system, horses were given even shots at winning by an elaborate system which paid far less for picking a favorite than a "long shot." Since then, bookmakers have generally stood by their bets while unfortunate bettors frequently skip town.

Gamblers were soon at the business of corrupting the races, though, by rigging them to their satisfaction. Doping and substituting horses was a common, though illegal, practice of mobster syndicates. A St. Louis-based syndicate called CAT once netted $10,000 a day at a string of American Midwest tracks. Racing in the United States was outlawed for a while until after World War I, and strict reforms followed. Today, even where state governments (as in Britain) have taken over the job of "making book" on the races, better deals can always be found by seeking the outlaw bookmaker who is still thriving on the odds at the track.

Bookmakers do not "book" only horse races, of course. They also make odds on other sporting events. This form of betting is more notorious than most. While gamblers may have considerable trouble beating the house on fair odds, they may be more fortunate in beating the spreads in games, or the odds in fights, if they can exert some influence on the participants in those contests. As a result, "fixing" fights and games has been common since the middle of the 19th century. The muscle needed for this sort of persuasion usually came from mobsters; and while

At faro and other such games, the dealer had all the advantages, often assisting the odds by arranging the cards in the house's favor. (By Thomas Francis Beard, from Harper's Weekly, February 23, 1867)

this activity has been curtailed since the 1930s, it always remains a potential source of income for the unscrupulous gambler.

Probably the most likely place to find 20th-century gamblers is in the casinos. The most famous of these is Monte Carlo in the small European nation of Monaco. In the United States, most casinos are found in Las Vegas, Nevada or Atlantic City, New Jersey. Professional American gamblers of the previous century, though, were not accustomed to such controlled and luxurious surroundings as were common in Europe. With the movement west in search of gold and silver, they joined the action in an attempt to pick up some of the loose money that flowed so easily. The famous *riverboat gamblers* traveled up and down the Mississippi playing each other and anyone else who wanted in. Cards and dice were the most common games. Further west, mining towns became notorious for wild and bawdy goings-on at the local saloon. Professional gamblers frequented the saloons to play card games against any sitters-in. Many arguments over cheating or failure to pay debts were settled in arranged or spontaneous gunfights in or out of the saloon. But saloon owners themselves were not usually gamesters, and the action was handled mainly by traveling professional gamblers.

The most prosperous gamblers today are casino owners. They also hire other people to work the house, foremost being the *croupiers* who actually run the games. There are also *house managers* and teams of security personnel on staff. The gamblers themselves are people from all social classes, though they usually make pretenses to being "high-society," as is the custom in the profession, owing to the European heritage of the great house gamblers. Many authorities believe that gamblers as a class are neurotic-obsessive people, compelled to gamble as much as an alcoholic is compelled to drink. Indeed, there is a *Gamblers Anonymous Association* to help them become independent of the vice. But most of the big money professionals are exact and calculating in their jobs and know when to "lay-off" as well as when to "jumpin." The image of the suicidal, down-and-out, bet-on-anything gambler is not an inaccurate one, but usually pertains to small-time bettors who are hopelessly outclassed by a formidable establishment of gamesters, racketeers, and bookmakers.

For related occupations in this volume, *Warriors and Adventurers*, see the following:
    Robbers and Other Criminals

For related occupations in other volumes of the series, see the following:
in *Financiers and Traders*:
    Bankers and Financiers
in *Manufacturers and Miners*:
    Miners and Quarriers
in *Performers and Players*:
    Athletes
    Sports Officials
    Racers
in *Restaurateurs and Innkeepers*:
    Innkeepers

Robbers and Other Criminals

In primitive societies, criminal acts are nearly always isolated violations of tribal rules. Only in civilized regions do some individuals step outside of the social framework and become *outlaws* by profession.

Theft, in one of its many forms, is the most widespread occupation for professional *criminals*. Whether practicing banditry in rural areas or sophisticated urban burglary, the *robber* pursued a hazardous career. In every culture, the risk of apprehension and punishment was always a real one. Depending on the nature of the crime and local customs, penalties could be severe. In many societies, even minor theft was an offense punishable by death. In others, imprisonment, torture, branding, flogging, deportation, or fines might be levied on the captured criminal.

In the Near East, the rise of cities—where large

numbers of people and their possessions were concentrated for the first time—made robbery a profitable career. The growth of a criminal underclass was a consequence of urbanization, a pattern that would be repeated countless times in different cultures across the centuries.

When Hammurabi codified the laws of ancient Babylonia in the 18th century B.C., he felt it necessary to devote a substantial section to the control of thieves. Robbery by day was a lesser crime, punishable by fines. *Burglars* working under cover of darkness, or those operating as *highwaymen*, robbing travelers, faced immediate execution if caught. Inns and drinking houses were the main haunts of the Babylonian criminal, and the same connection would hold true for many other cultures. *Tavern keepers* were required by law to report any people using their premises to plot criminal activity. It is doubtful that the section of Hammurabi's code concerning theft was any more successful than many later, unenforceable provisions of other legal codes.

In Egypt, too, theft was a standard component of society, with a widespread network of professional thieves and *fences*, who bought stolen goods for a fraction of their value. Individual criminals operated on their own in many cases, but organized theft was also present, sometimes aided and abetted by corrupt *government officials*.

The immense wealth commonly buried with pharaohs and noblemen was a lure which led to the organization of major gangs of *temple* and *tomb robbers* by 1100 B.C. They were often composed of the same skilled *workers* who had constructed the supposedly inviolate sanctuaries. A typical gang included *stonecutters*, *masons*, and *laborers* drawn from the temple work force, who knew what was available and had ready access to the tools and skills needed for successful break-ins. Government officials—including at times the prince of the *kher*, the man in charge of the entire necropolis ("city of the dead," or cemetery)—were often involved. *Scribes, temple priests*, and others drawn from the ranks of highly respectable citizens frequently joined in the illegal forays.

The rigid social stratification which developed in India extended to professional thieves as well. By 200 B.C., robbers formed a special caste whose members regarded themselves as "artists" and were duty bound to steal for a living. There were many thieves in the crowded Indian cities, and they were a determined lot. Common methods of breaking and entering involved boring through the walls to reach valuable goods. When discovered in the act, Indian thieves fought violently to avoid capture. In secluded forest areas, bandit gangs preyed on travelers, seeking either ransom or whatever valuables they could find on their victims. Often they would throw their victims into deep pits while they fleeced them or held them for ransom. In rural areas, local people often aided travelers, banging on pots and pans to bring help running. During some periods the central government kept down the incidence of crime by arranging for patrols on the road; the *dacoits* (robber gangs) themselves were often pressed into this service, acting as guards where once they had plundered.

The penalty that the Indian thief risked was death. A captured criminal was bound and garlanded with a ritual necklace of red flowers symbolizing death, and then had his head coated with red brick dust. The condemned prisoner was flogged with a thorn stick at every crossroads on the way to the execution ground. If still alive after a thousand strokes, the thief was impaled and left for the vultures.

Beggars also aligned themselves into a distinct urban class, operating a lucrative trade. About 40 percent of the

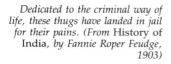

Dedicated to the criminal way of life, these thugs have landed in jail for their pains. (From History of India, *by Fannie Roper Feudge, 1903)*

begging population was able-bodied and relied on special clothes and makeup to create the impression of disease and deformity. As in many cultures, the use of children by professional beggars was widespread, since their vulnerable appearance could be counted on to inspire pity and prompt gifts of money. At the end of the day, the young apprentices would turn over their take to the older beggars and receive a small amount for their work.

Rome also harbored a substantial criminal class, in both the cities and the countryside. Taverns were notorious for the close and profitable relationships their proprietors were apt to have with local thieves. The taverns served both as headquarters and as spotting posts for potential victims. Outlaws invaded the countryside. Their ranks included the very poor, escaped slaves, and army deserters who had placed themselves outside any possible return to lawful society. One outlaw, a former slave himself and leader of a network of hundreds of robbers and informers, noted: "If masters treated their slaves better, there would be no robbers." Although travelers' purses were the main targets of many rural robbers, these ill-disciplined, impoverished gangs often acted as *rustlers*, making off with livestock. Robbers in this period were generally crucified, and some major highways were lined with rotting corpses left hanging as a warning to other potential criminals. Alternatively, they might be sent into the bloody gladiatorial circuses, in which they fought wild animals or each other to the death. After the fall of Rome, robbers continued to operate in Europe, but their numbers were considerably fewer, since travel and trade came largely to a standstill for some centuries.

Robbers continued to have good pickings in the Islamic world, which had its golden age when Europe was in deep decline. Bands of marauding nomads preyed on passing merchant caravans throughout Asia and northern Africa. Often such caravans would reach an accommodation with the local bandits, paying an agreed-upon amount to the outlaw chief in return for safe passage; sometimes one of the outlaws was sent along with the caravan as a "human passport," warning other robbers that the party had been granted immunity from attack.

In 1090 A.D. a branch of Shi'ite Moslems came into being in the Middle East which would gain lasting criminal fame. Their members, called *Assassins*, specialized in calculated murder. The Assassins were a dedicated band of terrorists linked by religious fervor and absolute loyalty to their leader, known as the Old Man of the Mountain. Assured of their entry into paradise if they were killed in a murder mission, Assassins were willing to sacrifice their lives whenever called for. This fearlessness, coupled with careful training in weapons, poison, and disguise, made them largely unstoppable. For nearly 200 years, the Assassins were a potent and feared political force in Persia and Iraq, basing their operations in several captured, heavily fortified castles. Though the organization was eventually destroyed by the Mongols, on their sweep through western Asia, its ideas spread and took hold. Indian *thugs* took inspiration partly from the terror tactics of the Assassins, and modern terrorist groups are in direct line of descent from these fanatical killers.

Meanwhile, as the Middle Ages wore on in Europe, large towns and cities were emerging. Feudal order and stability were unraveling, and landless people—discharged soldiers, rogues, and vagabonds—made travel through any countryside a hazardous undertaking. With the growing population and rise of a substantial merchant class, criminal careers underwent a rapid evolution from the isolated rural banditry that had been the rule.

In England, most professional criminals in the 14th century were *highwaymen*, who preyed on the many merchants traveling the roads of the kingdom. Highwaymen operated most commonly in small companies that were organized around a core of related robbers. In the absence of a strong central government the local gentry were laws unto themselves and

Highway robbers were often romanticized, like this 18th-century highwayman. (From Advertising Woodcuts from the Nineteenth-Century Stage, *by Stanley Appelbaum, Dover, 1977)*

maintained private armies to enforce their will upon anyone within reach. In this setting, some people became condemned outlaws simply because they had the misfortune to go against the wishes of the local lord. Not surprisingly, many people turned to careers as highwaymen to support themselves. They were rural criminals who laid claim to a heavily traveled section of road which lay alongside a wooded area that provided an easy and secure retreat. The fabled adventures of Robin Hood and his band of merry men were based on a common English lifestyle, though the gallantry and generosity attributed to them were notably lacking in the common robber band. Most led a rude and violent existence. As early as 1285, Edward I tried to halt robbery on the main highways by making property owners responsible for clearing the forests for 200 feet on each side of the road, destroying the favored hiding places of highwaymen.

In the cities different criminal careers were commonplace. Armed robbers were present, but more often a criminal would be a burglar relying on stealth and cunning to make a living. *Confidence men and swindlers* abounded in the cities and worked upon their credulous fellow citizens. A typical swindle of 1354 occurred in Barnstaple, Devon. Gervaise Worthy, Geoffrey Ipswich, and William Kyle called on the wife of one Roland Swalecomb, a wealthy merchant, while he was away on a business trip. They claimed to be converted pagans with magical powers and convinced her that they could double her wealth. Mrs. Swalecomb brought all the family valuables out of hiding—cups, belts, rings, and brooches of silver and gold. The three *con men* placed them first in a linen bag and then seemingly locked them securely in a strongbox. Taking the key, they told her that if she went to church and had three Masses a day celebrated for nine days, her treasure would magically double. At the end of that time she opened the box and found to her horror a bag filled with lead and stones, which had been skillfully substituted just before the locking. The three swindlers were caught, but managed to drag out their case so long that they were eventually found not guilty, a tactic still followed in our legal system.

Counterfeiting was another widespread crime in the Middle Ages, when the crudity of presses and widespread illiteracy made it an easy feat, even though it was considered treasonable and was punishable by death. Relatively few people worked as *counterfeiters* and those usually operated without helpers. This criminal career was open only to high-class, literate people with connections to royal clerks and officials. Most counterfeiters were either monks or ex-clerks themselves, who specialized in forgeries of the king's seal, which they then used or sold to obtain money and goods.

Urban crime evolved into a very special form in southern Spain. The *Garduna* was apparently the first society controlling large-scale organized crime. The founders of the Garduna were most emphatically not hill and country bandits. Known as *martens*—after the cunning fur-bearing relative of the weasel—they were the master burglars of cities, towns, and villages. Around 1482, the Catholic Church hired the Garduna to harass a Moslem people called the Moors in Spain. This was part of an infamous movement known as the Inquisition, aimed at identifying and punishing heretics, people who disagreed in any way with the Catholic Church's view. Ten years later, after the Moors were expelled from Spain, the Garduna turned their attention to the populace at large but retained their Inquisition contacts and used them to purchase protection from prosecution. The Garduna's close association with the government would last for more than 300 years.

The Garduna was unique in its orderly administration of criminal activity and in its coherence. Its members were fiercely loyal to the society; in return, the organization offered them the opportunity for excellent earnings and provided their families with a social-security system that was remarkable in its time. All profits from illegal activities were turned over to the boss of the Garduna and then divided up and distributed by him. He took a cut and then allocated one-third of the remaining money to the member who had provided the profits, one-third for pensions for the wives of dead and jailed members, and one-third for a general fund used for bribes. The security and attractiveness of society life made membership a sought-after commodity. Meticulous records were kept of the society's activities. Most of the Garduna's clients were priests and officers of the Inquisition. There were fixed rates for services rendered, and those were quite various. One-third of the priest-commissioned crimes involved the abduction of women, one-third involved assassination, and the remaining third was evenly spread among the other Garduna specialties, including robbery, maiming, false testimony, denunciation, and arson. Terms were always one-half payment in advance and the rest upon completion.

The Garduna was a bureaucracy of criminal specialists. Its ranks included criminals ranging from *ponteadores,* who were elite professional *killers* (the forerunners of modern *hit men*) to *hornets*, who were older men of respectable, dignified appearance who actually worked as *spotters* for burglars.

The Garduna's example spread to Naples with Spanish rule there in 1504, and an offshoot named the *Camorra* was the result. The Camorra was a unique society with its own special vocabulary, oral history, and ritual. It was formed in brigades (*brigata*) led by a captain (*capo*). All of the *capos* together formed the Grand Council, which made policy. Entry into the Camorra followed a period of apprenticeship. Novices were called *garzone di mala vita* and underwent a one-year probationary trial. They then became beginning members, *picciotto di szano*. The *picciotto* took an oath on crossed swords with his hands immersed in his own blood that he would be faithful to his comrades, would not deal with the police, would never denounce a member, and would never have recourse to the law. Members were also forbidden to reveal secrets about the Camorra, defraud the society of its gains, or violate any member's wife. The penalty for any infraction was a simple one: death. A *picciotto* became a full member of the Camorra only after he had committed an ordered murder, thus affirming his loyalty and placing himself irrevocably outside the law.

Naples was controlled by the Spanish Bourbons for much of the 18th and 19th centuries, but the Spanish were content to leave the affairs of the Naples government completely alone, so long as they received regular tax payments. The Camorra quickly moved into control and collected the Spanish taxes regularly. They virtually ruled Naples for 135 years and branched out into many legitimate and profitable enterprises to complement their criminal ones. Their rule was broken only after an organized civil war, led by some thousands of troops in the Italian army in 1863; after that, the Camorra reverted to a more limited local criminal band.

Professional criminals in many countries of Europe were organized and stratified. In Russia, for example, such diverse criminal workers as beggars and horse thieves had professional guilds. Each was headed by a guildmaster, trained apprentices in the tricks of the trade, and had its own secret language and customs. By some accounts, modern Russia continues to have a similar tight-knit criminal organization operating within its borders, but information on its activity is very sketchy.

Professional crime in England never acquired the closed superstructure of control and loyalty that the Spanish Garduna and the Neapolitan Camorra had. An underworld of *pickpockets*, thieves, robbers, swindlers, *extortionists*, and *prostitutes* existed, primarily in the cities, but they rarely came together in disciplined organizations. English criminals were transformed from a subculture to a major class of people by the upheaval in social conditions brought about by the Industrial Revolution in the 18th and 19th centuries. England, particularly London, produced a huge and distinct criminal class, which employed every member of many families in illegal activities.

There was a seemingly infinite gradation of specialties within the criminal community. *Mobsmen*—also known as the *light-fingered gentry*—plundered using their manual dexterity. The most respected practitioners of this field were the *swell mob*, high-class pickpockets of impeccable appearance who mingled with the rich. *Buzzers* extracted expensive lace handkerchiefs from gentlemen's pockets. *Wires* preyed on the pockets of ladies. *Proprailers* stole brooches and pins, while *thimblescrewers* specialized in separating watches from the chains meant to guard them. *Shoplifters* often wore voluminous clothing liberally supplied with hidden hooks and pockets for removing objects from stores. Another major field of criminal occupation was that of the *sneaksman*, who plundered by means of stealth. *Cracksmen* were elite skilled burglars. They were followed by *dragsneaks*, who stole from carts and coaches; *snoozers*, who slept at railroad hotels and left with other people's luggage in the early morning; *starglazers*, who cut panes from shop windows; and *noisy racket men*, who stole china and glass from outside store

displays. At the very bottom of the criminal hierarchy were lowly crooks like the *pudding snammer*, who stole food from people leaving cook shops, and the common *beggar*.

The poorest section of a city was called a *rookery*; until the end of the 19th century this was synonymous with the thieves' quarter, dire poverty and criminality often being closely allied. St. Giles was the great London rookery and was a warren of dingy alleyways and extreme poverty. Gang and criminal headquarters, known as *flash houses*, were nestled deep within the rookery in cheap inns and taverns.

Many thieves had a regular schedule of travel, wintering in London and then making a spring circuit through the countryside. These robbers were known as *trampers*, a name which has given us the modern *tramp*, complete with disreputable connotations. The English vagrant was most often a thief. The swell mob also made seasonal journeys, but their circuit followed the gentry's rounds from spa to spa.

Popular literature glorified criminal careers, and works such as Daniel Defoe's 1724 *John Sheppard* and a spate of stories about a character named Dick Turpin had youthful criminals as their heroes. Children entered careers of crime very early. Eight -year -olds were commonly hired out by their parents to professional beggars at fixed rates, depending on whether or not food was to be supplied. Crippled children were in great demand and brought premium rates. Young children were also valuable to thieves. London boasted several professional schools for the training of youthful thieves and pickpockets; these served as the model for Fagin's operation in Charles Dickens's *Oliver Twist*.

The huge amount of theft required the services of *fences* to receive stolen goods and resell them. The first person known to operate as a fence on a large scale was Jonathan Wild in London. He organized a district association of thieves and took a percentage of their take, in return for fencing their goods. His profits were large enough to provide for the purchase of a sloop, which he then used for trading stolen jewelry, banknotes, and plate, valuable dishes, often covered with gold or silver. By the time he was hanged in 1825, fencing was a major

Oliver Twist was not alone; these Italian boys are being forced to beg and steal for the masters who control them. (By A. Goult and B. Mayrand, from Harper's Weekly, *September 13, 1873)*

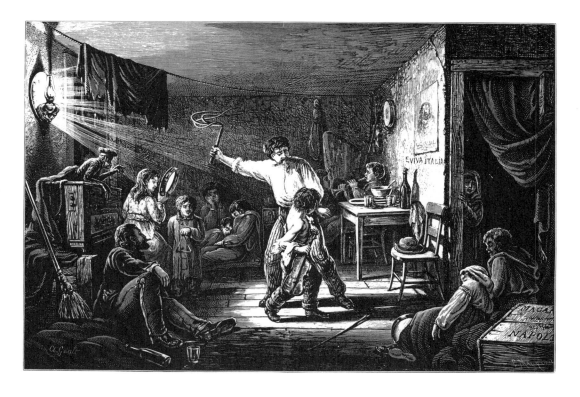

industry. The lowest fences were the operators of *dolly shops*, where stolen clothing, books, tools, and sundries were sold to the poor, with the thief receiving one-eighth of their value. By 1862, the first major study of crime in London counted 2,843 fencing operations in the city.

Licensed pawnbrokers served a legitimate function for the poor, allowing them to convert items of value into cash. But, since the pawnbrokers knew nothing of the source of these items, their services were often used by thieves, as well. Pawnbrokers would, for example, generally pay one-quarter of the value of jewelry and watches.

Criminal careers in England often ended in arrest, but jail was not the only prospect that the convict could anticipate. Transportation to British colonies and sentences of forced labor in the development of their resources were common punishments. North America was the major destination for convicts before 1776; after the American Revolution, Australia became the prime receiving station for English criminals. Those who survived the voyage and immediate adjustment to a new life rarely continued criminal occupations, but often became law-abiding citizenry of their new country.

In the United States the unexplored, spacious country, with many opportunities for the poor, acted against the establishment of a permanent urban criminal class such as that which existed in England. American cities had their share of swindlers, robbers, and prostitutes, but they were individuals, rather than members of a stagnant class. Professional criminals were a small and specialized population. Many American criminals were *sneak thieves*, who stole from houses and banks. *Bank sneaks* often worked in gangs, using a lookout, a diversionary team, and an actual *grabber* to make their hauls. *House sneaks* were basically urban crooks. By the mid-19th century, they had developed skeleton keys and jimmies (a type of crowbar used to pry open windows and doors) as the major tools of their trade. Shoplifters, or *boosters*, were also common in the cities, working in much the same way as their English counterparts.

For people who have lived outside of society's conventions and laws, confinement in prison, as here in the exercise yard of Newgate, comes doubly hard. (By Gustave Doré, from London: A Pilgrimage, *1872)*

After the American Civil War, new forms of criminal activity became current in a country filled with ex-soldiers trained in the use of guns and the handling of explosives. *Safecracking* became a criminal specialty with the invention of dynamite and nitroglycerine. *Train robbery* also became a common criminal occupation; the first one took place in 1866, when John and Simon Reno took $13,000 from an Ohio and Mississippi train safe. Armed robbery of stagecoaches, banks, and individuals was the characteristic crime of the American West before organized law enforcement became effective in the 20th century. Outlaw communities sprang up in remote sanctuaries, such as Brown's Hole at the junction of Colorado, Utah and Wyoming, where Butch Cassidy and the Wild Bunch made their base. These were rude towns with limited life spans, disappearing as soon as law enforcement made serious inroads on their territory.

The unsettled nature of the American frontier also made it a rich hunting ground for professional crooked *gamblers*, who relied on carefully polished routines of manual dexterity to take the element of chance out of card games. By inserting hidden cards into a deal, marking decks, and switching cards without being seen, they could go from town to town winning enough to support their life-styles without exciting too much suspicion. Gamblers often worked alone but they sometimes employed a partner, who would either serve to distract other players' attentions or subtly tip off the values of their hands. The professional gamblers often dressed the part, wearing clothes that were distinctly citified and in sharp contrast to the rough working clothes common on the Western frontier. A small concealed gun called a *derringer* was often part of the outfit and was sometimes used with deadly effect to put a stop to the protests of an aggrieved loser.

The world of the traveling American circus bred distinctive criminal professionals called *grifters*, or *confidence men*. These people originally specialized in the rigged games of chance, such as three-card monte, which were important parts of every circus sideshow. Their activities were criminal, but circus grifting went on with the total understanding and protection of circus management. Its practitioners developed a very strong sense of superiority over the *marks* (victims), who allowed themselves to be taken in their search for easy money. Grifting soon shed its circus dependency. In 1867, an enterprising grifter named Ben Marks set up the first "Big Store" in Cheyenne, Wyoming. This operation had the appearance of a normal shop on the outside but steered its customers into a large-scale series of three-card monte games in back rooms.

The trade soon developed into what its operatives viewed as a criminal art form; it depended on highly skilled professionals, who combined acting and persuasive ability and avoided the use of force entirely. Men and women grifters worked around the country, favoring urban locations, where there were many opportunities, but also operating in small towns as well. Extremely elaborate cons were sometimes employed involving dozens of grifters, who were assembled from the floating ranks of the profession for that single occasion. Utterly realistic betting parlors, stockbrokers' offices, or prize fights were staged in order to get a wealthy mark to commit large sums of money to the swindle. When done properly, the con was uncontested by the victim.

During the 1930s, *bank robbery* by gangs of criminals acquired widespread notoriety. Robbers like John Dillinger and Bonnie and Clyde gained national prominence and became folk heroes to some degree. Throughout the 20th century, *organized crime* has come to control much of the highly lucrative gambling, extortion, prostitution, and narcotics trade in the United States. The *Mafia*, a lineal descendant of the Italian Camorra, developed a massive, highly disciplined structure of professional criminals who operated entirely outside the law. Each family, or gang, relied on a network of lieutenants and soldiers to enforce the policy decisions reached by its leadership, often a single man. As criminal profits grew, a good portion was often reinvested in legitimate business operations, which served both as profit-making enterprises and as a diversionary tactic to cloud illegal activities. In recent years, the control of some sections of the lucrative criminal field has passed into the hands of gangs of professional criminals of different nationalities. The drug trade in cocaine and marijuana from South America, for example, is now handled in large part by Colombian nationals.

Much of the criminal activity in the United States and other countries is carried out by an unorganized subculture of the poor. Ill-educated and unskilled, many drift into criminal occupations after a youthful arrest. As they grow older, their lives become a series of criminal actions regularly punctuated by repeated arrests and imprisonment.

In most societies, a two-tiered division of criminals exists. At the upper end are *white-collar criminals*, typically well-educated business people engaged in illegal business practices and *embezzlement*, and top professional robbers of various descriptions. These elite criminals pay careful attention to the details of their crimes and often invest large sums of capital to secure massive returns on their illegal activities. Some have used computer skills to commit *electronic theft*, transferring funds from other accounts, while others have planned and executed intricately choreographed robberies.

At the other end of the spectrum are the great majority of criminals. Generally drawn from the poor, they often act impulsively and go after targets of relatively little value. A small-time house thief may terrorize one neighborhood, for instance, randomly going from house to house, until tracked down by law-enforcement agencies. Though a fringe occupation that exists outside the frameworks of organized societies, crime in its various forms seems guaranteed a continuing role in most human communities.

For related occupations in this volume, *Warriors and Adventurers*, see the following:
    Gamblers and Gamesters
    Soldiers

For related occupations in other volumes of the series, see the following:
in *Builders*:
    Construction Laborers
    Masons
in *Communicators*:
    Clerks
    Messengers and Couriers
    Printers
    Scribes

in *Financiers and Traders*:
    Bankers and Financiers
    Merchants and Shopkeepers
in *Helpers and Aides*:
    Undertakers
in *Leaders and Lawyers*:
    Judges
    Lawyers
    Police Officers
    Political Leaders
    Prison Guards and Executioners
in *Performers and Players* (forthcoming):
    Variety Performers
in *Restaurateurs and Innkeepers* (forthcoming):
    Innkeepers
    Prostitutes
in *Scholars and Priests* (forthcoming):
    Monks and Nuns
    Priests

Sailors

The sea has always fascinated people. Many have fallen passionately in love with its glamour and mystery. Others have just as passionately feared its vastness and its often treacherous nature. The sea has a lore all its own and a major place in the history of occupations. Many people wedded to the land have viewed oceans essentially as boundaries, but those able to sail ships have seen the seas as both a source of food and a path to lucrative commerce and military success.

Sailors have always combined various occupations in one, being by turn *merchants, fishers, soldiers, shipwrights, pirates, sail makers, pilots,* and *navigators*; most of these fields are treated in separate articles.

Occupations on the high seas have followed an interesting evolution. Obtaining food from the sea probably was what first caused people to launch boats, and fishing remains a major industry to this day. The vast majority of sailors throughout history have been involved in some way with the mercantile trade. Most sailors have had to be workers on the ship first and *soldiers, merchants,* or *pirates* second. Of course, some governments, such as that of ancient Rome, have sent ships to sea with contingents of soldiers whose only real task was to fight the enemy. These soldiers were essentially *marines,* starting a long tradition that continues today. Whatever their specialties, sailors have always had a rough life on the sea, at the mercy of storms and a variety of debilitating diseases.

The first ships were certainly crude craft—little more than hollowed-out logs, operated by *rowers* or *polers.* Some simple craft show a remarkable amount of sophistication and perfect adaptation to a specific environment. The Eskimo *kayak* is a perfect example. The kayak has a frame of wood or whalebone with a skin stretched over it. The Eskimo kneels inside a type of enclosed cockpit and uses a double-bladed paddle to propel the craft through the water. With a boat like this—which weighs only about 60 pounds—the Eskimo has an excellent craft for hunting or travel.

After the dugouts and the various types of canoes, crafts such as the ancient Egyptian reed and papyrus boats were constructed. None of these boats were really good fighting craft, but once they became larger, and more rowers were added, people discovered that they could add a platform to these boats to hold soldiers. So the fighting ship was born.

The sea as a major highway for commerce is certainly an ancient concept. The Egyptians were trading over the Mediterranean with other Middle Eastern kingdoms by 3400 B.C. By 3000 B.C. the Sumerians in Mesopotamia were building temples made of teak that came from southwest India, wood that was presumably brought by coastal traders by sea. Indian and later Indo-Malayan traders seemed to have opened up sea routes to the East by a very early date.

Nearer to historical times, the Phoenicians were some of

Egyptians took advantage of a strong northerly wind by using both sails and oars on their ships. (By Manning de V. Lee, from Historic Ships, by Rupert Sargent Holland, 1926)

the greatest sailors. Tradition has it that they came originally from the Persian Gulf, home of the ancient Mesopotamian-Indian trade. By a thousand years B.C., the Phoenicians were certainly accomplished sailors. They had sailed an area known as Tarshis (variously placed in Asia Minor, Iberia, and even Malaya) with King Solomon of Israel; they are reported to have sailed around Africa from east to west (as are some Greeks); they had explored the entire Mediterranean; and they had even pushed out into the Atlantic Ocean, possibly reaching southern Britain and probably pushing down the western coast of Africa. Most of this activity was in search of trade goods, mostly precious metals, notably the tin vital for making bronze. These *merchant-sailors* generally conducted their trade in the age-old fashion of *dumb* or *silent barter*. That is, they would signal their arrival by a smoking fire on the beach, and then wordlessly and without direct contact offer piles of goods and accept equivalent piles of goods in return.

Trade was equally active in the Indian Ocean. The Chinese may have invented the *compass* as an aid to navigation as early as 2600 B.C., but they were, in truth, not fervent sailors. Throughout much of history, Indian and Indo-Malayan sailors carried on the trade of the

Spice Route, along the southern coast of Asia, bearing spices and other precious goods, notably gems and metals, and later silks. Though these traders initially followed the coastline, they early began to cross the open water, using birds to guide them, and later judging their position by the stars. By the time the Greeks arrived on the scene to trade in India themselves, they were astonished at the amount of trading already going on. In the first century B.C., an anonymous Greek mariner wrote the *Periplus of the Erythraean* (Red) *Sea*, in which he noted that Arabian ports were busy with merchants. Of one of them he said:

> . . . the whole place is crowded with Arab shipowners and seafaring men, and is busy with the affairs of commerce; for they carry on a trade with the farside coast [Africa] and with Barygaza [in India], sending their own ships there.

Harbor pilots guided trading ships into special anchorages set aside for them, and goods were off-loaded onto barges in the main ports. An Indian poet of the third century B.C. described the scene:

> . . . sacks of pepper are brought from the houses to the market; the gold received from ships, in exchange for articles sold, is brought to shore in barges . . . and . . . [the king] presents to visitors the rare products of the seas and mountains.

Sharing in all this activity were *pirates*, who operated on the Spice Route for thousands of years, especially at the tip of Malaya, in the Persian Gulf and Red Sea, and in the many groups of islands along the route.

Pirates were also prevalent in the Mediterranean. Indeed, in much of the sea's early history, merchant-sailors and pirates were virtually indistinguishable. The Greeks often branded their trading rivals, the Phoenicians, as pirates, but the great Aristotle considered piracy so much the norm that he classed the occupation as a form of hunt-

This Eastern sailor is being hauled back on board, cheating the large shark on the right of its prey. (From Borobudur, Java, eighth century A.D.)

ing. The fifth-century B.C. Greek historian Thucydides described how it works:

> For the Grecians in old time, and of the barbarians both those on the continent who lived near the sea, and all who inhabited islands, after they began to cross over more commonly to one another in ships, turned to piracy, under the conduct of their most powerful men, with a view both to their own gain, and to maintenance for the needy, and falling upon towns that were unfortified, and inhabited like villages, they rifled them, and made most of their livelihood by this means; as this employment did not yet involve any disgrace, but rather brought with it somewhat of glory.

Piracy of this sort continued throughout history, flowering at any time when strong control was lacking over the sea routes. But, as Thucydides implies, the Greeks, and

Many early sailors were fishers, like these on the Sea of Galilee. (From Picturesque Palestine, *19th century)*

the Phoenicians as well, settled down gradually to more respectable trading, though they often fought each other in the process.

Ships with sails were used on all these main trading routes, but on the Mediterranean the general calmness of the sea and uncertainty of winds made oars a necessary supplement to sail power. The main type of ship in the Mediterranean was the *galley*, a fast, highly maneuverable craft. The basic design consisted of a long, sleek hull, propelled primarily by twin banks of oars on either side of the ship. Galleys also carried square sails.

The galley was the queen of the Mediterranean. It was the basic warship, the tool of empire for every power in the area. Many sailing powers—including the Phoenicians, Greeks, Romans, Carthaginians, Byzantines, Arabs, Turks, Venetians, Spanish, among others—sought to control the sea with their galley fleets. This remarkable ship, introduced in about the eighth century B.C., was used in battle as late as 1790. That means that the same type of vessel was in service for nearly 3,000 years! These ships were highly maneuverable and quite deadly on a relatively calm stretch of water. The galley was a ship of the inland seas; it could not really challenge the changeable oceans.

The basic war galley had a row of oars on each side; a typical early Greek galley had 50 oars—25 on each side. The main armament of the galley was its metal beak or ram, which was fitted on the bow. The purpose of the ram was to sink enemy ships. The *captain* of the galley would try to position his ship so the front beak could slice amidships into an enemy vessel and cut through beneath the water line. He would give the order and the rowers would increase their tempo and sail toward the enemy. Once the ships had collided, the attacker would pull away, leaving the crippled enemy vessel to fill with seawater and sink.

Since it was extremely difficult structurally to build a very long galley, designers took a different tack; they built upwards. As decks were added, the *bireme*—a galley with two decks of rowers—and the *trireme*—a ship with three decks—were invented. The additional rowers added power and speed, and the ship itself was heavier and better able to ram opposing ships.

Several different categories of people operated these ships. Since the galleys were primarily used as warships, they carried *soldiers*, who did the actual fighting; these were, in essence, *marines*. A paid crew, led by officers, operated the sail and made repairs. Finally there were the *rowers*.

The rowers were never very well off in the scheme of things, but their fates differed drastically, depending on which masters they served. For example, the Greek rowers were freemen and carried arms. However, many of the Middle Eastern, African, Asian, and some other European countries later used *slaves* and *criminals* to row the galleys. These galley slaves led a miserable existence. They were chained to their oars and lived in filth. Death was often a release—and it came frequently. When *pirates* or warships attacked, the rows of oars were the most tempting targets. It was only logical: Disable the rowers and you halt the ship. And if the ship was rammed and sank, the unfortunate rowers often went down with the galley.

The galley has been used in some of the most momentous sea battles of all time. One of the first came during the Greco-Persian War at the Battle of Salamis fought in 480 B.C. This naval engagement decided the fate of Greece. The Persians had already annihilated the small Greek army at Thermopylae and captured Athens. The Persians still faced a large Greek fleet composed of ships from many different city-states. The Persian fleet was composed of ships manned by sailors from many countries within the empire—Phoenicians, Egyptians, and even Ionian Greeks, from islands ruled by the Persian emperor Xerxes.

Except for ramming techniques, sea battles at this time were much like land engagements. The Greek ships carried heavily armed soldiers called *hoplites*, while the Persians relied upon their more lightly armored *archers*. The Greek goal was clear—close with the enemy ships

Galleys descended from this Greek one of 700 B.C. sailed the Mediterranean for over 2,000 years. (By Manning de V. Lee, from Historic Ships, *by Rupert Sargent Holland, 1926)*

and then capture them by boarding and engaging in hand-to-hand combat. The Persians, on the other hand, wanted to avoid closing, relying first upon long-range archery, and then ramming the Greek ships.

The Greeks won the first round at Salamis even before the battle began. A *double agent* convinced the Persian ruler, Xerxes, that the Athenians were ready to desert the Greek fleet and that the Greeks were in chaos. This persuaded Xerxes to order his fleet to engage the Greeks in an area unfavorable to the Persians—a narrow strait, through which the Persians had to pass. As they did, their ships became bunched up, so their numbers did not help them. The resulting fight was won by the Greeks, since they were able to bear down upon the Persians and force them to fight their hoplites. By the end of the battle, the Greeks had lost 40 ships while the Persians had lost 200 and any chance of conquering Greece.

As the centuries passed, little changed in the design of the galley or the occupations within it. Since the Romans were not sailors, they lost some of their early sea battles with the vastly more experienced Carthaginians (descendants of the Phoenicians). The Carthaginian ships were far more maneuverable than the Roman or even Greek galleys. The Romans cleverly tried to even the odds, first by copying the basic Carthaginian ship design and then by figuring out a way to fight the battles to their advantage.

Like the Greeks, the Romans' greatest asset was the heavily armed soldier, so Roman designers increased the number of soldiers each galley could hold and created a method of getting these soldiers into ship-to-ship combat more quickly. This was accomplished by means of a device called the *corvus* (raven). Essentially, it was a type of gangplank that was dropped onto the enemy ship. A large spike at the tip of the corvus would dig into the enemy's deck and hold it firmly while Roman soldiers would swarm across and take the enemy in hand-to-hand fighting. The Romans used the corvus successfully to engage Carthaginian ships. Despite innovations in fighting techniques, however, the ships of this time—no matter how streamlined or what better type of rowing method was introduced—were still galleys.

More than a thousand years later, the Mediterranean was still witnessing great sea battles fought with galleys. The Battle of Lepanto, in 1571, pitted the forces of Christendom—Spain, Venice, the Papal States, and other allies—against the Moslem forces of Turkey. Despite the continued use of galleys, there were some major differences between this battle and the sea battles of the ancient world. Guns were used, and a few new types of ships had come onto the scene, notably large sailing vessels called *galleons* and *galleases*. Galleons were large ships with three masts and at least two decks. Galleases were a cross between galleys and galleons. The galleases were larger and carried more guns, but they still had to be rowed to battle. The Lepanto engagement was bloody and furious. Each force had more than 200 ships. In the end, the Holy League, as the Christians were referred to, defeated the Turks. It was still primarily a battle of ramming and hand-to-hand combat. Yet the added dimension of gunpowder and cannon pointed to a new form of ship combat—and a new type of occupation, the *gunner*. Many of the ships carried cannons and many of the soldier-sailors—especially on the Christian side—used firearms. The real winners of the battle were the thousands of Christian galley slaves who were liberated after the capture of many Turkish ships.

During the Dark Ages after the fall of Rome, northern European waters were dominated by Scandinavian sailors called Vikings. As much soldiers as sailors, the Vikings were fearless traders, fighters, and explorers. They burst onto the European scene in the late eighth century, when their *longships* raided rich monasteries and sacked towns. Eventually, their longships reached the British Isles, Ireland, Western Europe, the Mediterranean, Russia, Iceland, Greenland, and Vinland—somewhere in North America. The Vikings

As sailors moved into unknown waters, they often saw the seas as peopled with an unending variety of fearsome creatures. (From Cosmographia, *by Sebastian Munster, 1550, Staatliche Museen zu Berlin)*

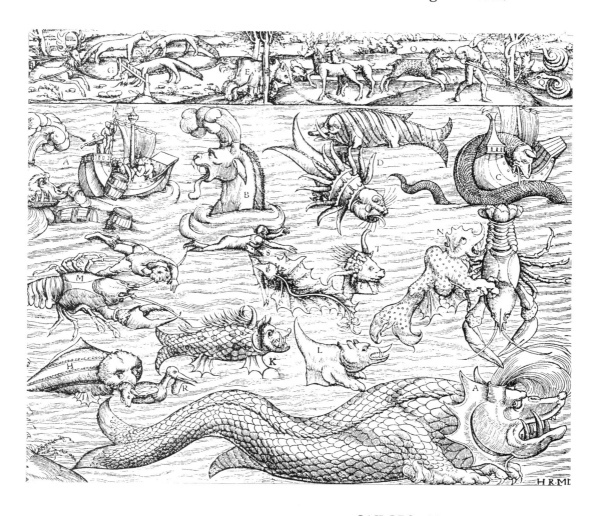

carved out kingdoms in many European countries for they were also settlers and traders.

In many ways, the Viking longship or *drakkar* (dragonship) was similar to the galley. It was an oared vessel with a square sail. However, the longship was far sturdier than the galley, and the rowers were all warriors. These ships were extremely well built—otherwise they could never have made so many long-distance voyages across the rough Atlantic. The Viking sailors were just as rugged as their ships. The longships had no decks, so the crew was constantly exposed to the elements, which could be quite fierce in the northern seas.

The Viking longship was the model copied by other Europeans. Alfred the Great, king of England, built the first English navy in order to counter the Vikings. His builders copied the design of the longship, and this fleet had many successes against invading fleets. In 1066, when William the Conqueror—successor to the Viking-Norman tradition—launched his attack on England, he used ships which closely followed the longship lines.

Sailing in the East

While the Mediterranean and European waters were largely given over to sea raiders, regular trade flourished in the Indian Ocean. On land the Moslems were militaristic, but on the sea they were far more interested in trade. Moslem ships fanned out along the coast of Africa and all along southern Asia. Often these ships were manned by the traditional sailors and traders in the area—Indians, Syrians, Jews, and even some Greeks. In the ninth century, Jewish traders routinely crossed from France to the Suez, overland to the Red Sea, and then by ship to India and all the way to China and back, sometimes detouring to Constantinople to sell their goods, unless they headed straight back to France. The sea trade with China was highly regulated (and would remain so into modern times), as an anonymous Arabic author noted in *Akhbar al-Sin w-al-Hind*:

> When the seamen come in from the sea, the Chinese seize their goods and put them in the sheds; there they guard them securely for [up to] six months, until the last seaman has come in. After that, three-tenths of every consignment is taken as a duty, and the remainder is delivered to the merchants. Whatever the Government requires, it takes at the highest price and pays for promptly and fairly.

Even in their literature the Arabs honored sea traders. The legendary Sindbad the Sailor—whose story combines and heightens the experience of real Arab sailors—was a merchant. As the tale is told in the *Arabian Nights*, Sindbad bought himself a load of goods and then went to the docks, found a ship that he liked, bought it, and hired a crew, employing some of his slaves and servants as *inspectors*.

The Chinese themselves did very little sailing. In the 15th century, under the Ming dynasty, they sent a series of successful expeditions to western Asia and Africa, gathering much tribute. But they withdrew from seagoing activity, preferring to rely on others to carry on the marine trade. Later, when the Europeans arrived on the scene, they simply continued an ancient sea-trading tradition in the region.

One of the constants in these southern Asian waters was the presence of active pirates. From all the coasts, from the many islands, from reefs and rocky points, they operated. Marco Polo, who returned by sea from China to Venice, described vividly how these pirates—who sailed with their whole families, including women and children—cruised in a line, a few miles apart, together covering perhaps 100 miles of sea. When one sighted a merchant ship, he signaled the others with beacons, and all the pirates then gathered around. Generally they took only goods, letting the merchants go free, so · that—they said—the traders could return again with more cargo.

A New Age

Meanwhile in Europe, trade began to flourish once again in the later Middle Ages. Ship design improved. The addition of the triangular *lateen* sail, introduced to the Mediterranean by the Moslems, allowed the development of larger ships that relied totally upon sails, especially in the northern European waters where winds were found more consistently than in the Mediterranean. The improvements fed and were fed by the ever-increasing strength of a federation of German towns, called the *Hanseatic League*. The Hanseatic members were free and independent cities which formed a trading network around the Baltic and North seas. Between the 14th and 17th centuries they controlled most northern European trade in their network.

To handle this increasing trade, larger merchant ships were built. The primary type of ship was the *cog*. Single-masted and wide, cogs were in the range of 300 tons. Not nearly as maneuverable as the Viking longship, these ships, often called *roundships*, still effectively spread trade throughout Europe. Later, the single-masted cog was replaced by first twin-masted and then triple-masted *carracks*, with somewhat larger tonnages. Another type of ship which became famous in the explorations that started in the 15th century was the *caravel*. Used at first for fishing, the caravel was fast and easily handled. Usually under 100 tons, these ships were very popular with explorers. Columbus's ships—the *Nina*, the *Pinta*, and the *Santa Maria*—were all caravels.

This was a very heady age for sailors. Ever more prosperous Europeans were demanding luxuries, such as silks and spices, which could be obtained from the distant East. The Portuguese and Spanish led the way in the development of ships and skills necessary to open new trade routes to the East. Prince Henry of Portugal gathered together *geographers, mathematicians*, and *astronomers* to help Portuguese sailors learn the art of navigation. He also sent out many small exploring parties to map the coast of Africa. By 1490, Portuguese

sailors had rounded the Cape of Good Hope and sailed into the Indian Ocean.

The 15th and 16th centuries witnessed the birth of powerful seagoing nations. Countries such as Portugal and Spain were joined by the Netherlands and England in the hectic competition to establish trade routes and annex colonies. Searches for new routes to India and China led to the discovery of the New World, which was subsequently divided among the competitors, including France, over the next two centuries.

In 1519, Ferdinand Magellan began his epic voyage of sailing around the world. His expedition began with 265 sailors—of whom only 19 lived to reach Spain again. Magellan himself was killed in the Philippines, but his second in command, Juan Sebastian de Elcano, continued the voyage. Despite the losses, this voyage was an immense success; it proved that a ship could actually sail around the world.

These longer voyages were extremely demanding on the crews. For many centuries, a host of diseases would plague the long-distance trading, exploring, and military ships. Cramped into tiny, often cold, and wet quarters, the common sailors died like flies. The long voyages around the southern capes and into the Far East introduced sailors to another disease: *scurvy*. This is caused by a dietary deficiency of vitamin C. Fresh fruits and vegetables could have prevented it, though sailors did not know it at the time; in any case, these perishable foods usually could not be carried aboard ship. In fact, the common sailor's diet was rarely more than hardtack—a type of biscuit—and salted meat. Crew after crew was lost to this dreaded disease.

The Dutch introduced one solution to the scurvy problem. They established a settlement at Capetown in South Africa, so ships on the way to the Spice Islands could stop to obtain fresh vegetables.

The real elimination of scurvy was due to the demonstration by Scottish navy surgeon James Lind in 1749 that fresh fruits and vegetables, especially oranges and lemons, could prevent the disease. By the end of the 18th century, British naval crews on long voyages were routinely given the juice of limes—a practice that gave rise to the nickname *Limey*, meaning Englishman.

The explorers, merchants and sea warriors of the Age of Discovery—from the 15th century to modern times—were the same people. It was common for sailors to move back and forth between the merchant marine and the navy of their country. In fact, sovereigns often commandeered merchant ships in time of war for their navies. In this period, the merchant ships had mounted guns and were well able to defend themselves from pirates and hostile competitive forces. However, times were quickly changing, and the need for professional military forces was recognized, especially in England.

England's navy was forged in wars with Spain and the Netherlands. Its first great sea battle was with the *Spanish Armada*. A new ship, the English galleon, here proved to be the most effective fighting ship in the world. Lower and faster than the high-castled Spanish ships, the English galleon outmaneuvered the Spanish craft and wreaked havoc with its superior gunnery. During the 17th century, the British established the Hudson's Bay company and the East India Company. Both proved to be very successful at extending England's dominance of sea trade to both East and West. England's navy crushed competitor after competitor through the 18th century, although challenged heavily by first the Dutch and then the French.

The British navy attracted officers from the highest classes in the country. It was common for the second sons of nobility to enter this respected profession, where they had a chance to gain fame and riches. It was far more difficult to obtain full crews, however. Until 1740, it was perfectly legal to take sailors—foreign or British—from any British ship and press them into service in the Royal Navy. In times of war, different localities were issued quotas of people they had to supply to the navy. Little wonder that these communities chose to offer *criminals* and other citizens of "little social value."

The Royal Navy tried to handle these recruits through brutal discipline. At times, though, discipline alone was not enough. In 1797, entire fleets mutinied at Spithead and Nore. These mutinies were particularly frightening to the British establishment, since they took place while the nation was at war, with the French.

British seamen had plenty to complain about: poor pay, which was often withheld; bad food, often rotten or crawling with weevils; and harsh discipline. Floggings were common; there was even a punishment called "flogging round the fleet," which consisted of the prisoner being given a dozen lashes on every ship in the fleet. Few survived. Finally, there was the general condition of life—rampant disease, terrible ventilation, little medicine. Conditions were so bad that ten times as many sailors died of disease as fell in battle. The mutinies were put down, and conditions did start to improve, continuing throughout the 19th century. However, flogging was not abolished until 1867. And *impressment* (forcing merchant sailors into the service of the Royal Navy) of suspected British subjects off United States ships was one of the major causes of the War of 1812.

Much of a sailor's time was traditionally spent in simply keeping the ship tidy, trim, and seaworthy. (By Gustave Doré, from London: A Pilgrimage, *1872)*

In the 17th and 18th centuries, wars among the European powers were common. Enterprising seamen could make a great deal of money by taking advantage of the fighting. *Privateers* became common. These were privately owned ships that were given permission to act as warships on behalf of a specific government. Essentially, this was permission to act legally as pirates. Little wonder that many privateers kept to their trade after the wars ended. In some cases, pirates and *buccaneers* (a Caribbean name for pirates) were even sought to become privateers.

The buccaneers in the Caribbean were the ones who inspired our romantic image of pirates. These were the infamous *swashbucklers* like Henry Morgan, Captain Kidd, and Edward Teach, better known as Blackbeard. Henry Morgan was probably the most successful buccaneer. Among his exploits was the sacking of Panama City in 1671. This impressed King Charles II of Britain, who offered Morgan the governorship of Jamaica. Captain Kidd began as a privateer and was very successful in preying on the French—and on other ships he was not supposed to attack. He was hanged in 1701.

Edward Teach, Blackbeard, was an extremely colorful and cruel pirate. Pictured with the ends of his mustache lighted, this pirate struck terror in the Caribbean. To obtain a safe base, he split his loot with the governor of North Carolina. Frightened people from that colony asked Virginia for help. In 1718, two Royal Navy sloops surprised Teach in the James River. Blackbeard was killed and his head was cut off.

Many pirates later moved from the Caribbean to the Indian Ocean. One group of ex-Caribbean pirates even formed the independent republic of Libertalia on the island of Madagascar. Other pirates continued operating in Eastern waters, as they had for generations.

The evolution in occupations aboard the sailing ships followed the evolution of the ships themselves. The purpose of the crew was to sail the ship and keep it in perfect working order. The smaller vessels did not need a large crew to maintain them, but as masts and sails were added and the ships became larger, more crew members were needed. To get top speed and the most efficient performance out of ships, a crew had to act as a team. Hauling down sails and raising them to get the perfect equation of sail to wind was very important. This was especially true in battle, when getting the wind gauge on an enemy could mean the difference between defeat and victory. The experience and sailing ability of the English crews—unwilling conscripts though they sometimes were—often made the difference in many naval engagements. While French and Spanish ships were often more powerful, they did not have crews or officers to match the English.

Aboard ship, a few experienced people practiced their crafts. *Sailmakers* and *carpenters* were on the larger ships, along with *coopers* (barrel makers) and *barbers*. Of course, the smaller ships would make do with as few individuals as possible, each trained in many skills.

On military ships, the hierarchy was rigid. There was a definite class structure which decided promotions. The best sailors were *able seamen*, as opposed to *ordinary seamen*, who were either impressed into service or were inexperienced adventurers who chose to go to sea. Under the captain of the ship would be several junior officers, lieutenants, and *midshipmen*. Midshipmen were often teenagers from good families, who expected to be promoted. Occasionally, promotions from the ranks made older men midshipmen. The older men did not often move further up in rank, but they had the special status of age. Other officers included the *surgeon*, the *chaplain*, and the *purser*. The purser was the man in charge of obtaining provisions for the ship. If he was good, the ship was well provided for. If, as was more likely, he was more interested in making deals with *provisioners* to line his own pockets, the ship suffered second-rate food.

There also were types of *noncommissioned officers* on board. These included men with valued skills, such as the *gunner*, the *master-at-arms*, and the *boatswain*, who was in charge of the deck, including crew, rigging, and anchors. An even more valued noncommissioned officer was the *master*. This individual was in charge of navigating the ship, obviously a vital job. Before the 18th century, navigation was more hit-and-miss than truly scientific. Boats had crude *compasses* and *quadrants*, along with

vague charts and maps to guide them. At best, these instruments—along with sighting the stars—would give the ship's officers good latitude discovery, but poor longitudinal sightings.

By the early 18th century, government bodies were offering prizes for effective navigational instruments. In 1731, John Hadley invented the *octant* and then, in 1757, the *sextant* was introduced. These instruments measured the altitude of celestial bodies, such as the Moon. Although they were not sophisticated by today's standards, these instruments demanded a high level of skill in the seaman using them. Gradually, the instruments were improved. By the 19th century officers

Chinese merchant-sailors took great commercial ships like these throughout Eastern waters. (New York Public Library, mid-19th century)

Sailors in difficulty at sea often depended on rescuers from the land, private individuals or coast guard. (Advertising woodcut from Little Em'ly, *London and New York, 1869, adapted from* David Copperfield, *by Charles Dickens)*

could use them, in conjunction with a *chronometer* (invented in 1735) and the *British Nautical Almanac*, to locate their positions as to latitude and longitude with a high degree of accuracy.

In the 18th and 19th centuries, ship designers were developing larger and faster ships to handle increased commerce around the world. There were two primary categories of ships: those built along traditional lines to carry as much cargo as possible at no great speed, and those built to carry smaller amounts of more precious cargo at top speed.

Americans led the way in designing and building small, fast ships. During the War of 1812, American ships were used to slip past the Royal Navy's blockade and to attack British shipping. After the war, the ships were in demand by pirates, privateers, *smugglers*, and *slavers*. In fact, wherever there was legal or illegal cargo to be transported, the American ships were used. Baltimore-built craft had the best reputation as fast, sweet-handling ships. At first, in the early years of the 1800s, these ships were quite small—between 200 and 300 tons. By mid-century these craft, now called *clipper ships*, had grown larger—more than 1,000 tons—and faster.

The California Gold Rush and the Asian tea trade provided clipper ships with two important markets. When gold was discovered at Sutter's Mill in 1849, a tremendous demand for passage to the West Coast was generated. Although it was more than 17,000 miles away around Cape Horn, many passengers found it faster and safer to reach California by clipper ship than to risk an overland voyage through some very wild territory in the West. A fast clipper ship could make the voyage in under 90 days. As the American clipper ships transported people and supplies to the West Coast, their owners made tremendous profits. However, there was still the problem of what to do with an empty clipper ship docked in San Francisco. The problem was partly solved in 1850 when Britain repealed the Navigation Act, which had required all imports into Britain to be carried by British ships or the ships of the exporting nation. Now the clipper ships were able to drop off Gold Rush cargo in California and then sail across the Pacific to China in order to pick up tea for Britain. They completed their around-the-world voyage by picking up another Gold Rush cargo in New York or some other East Coast port. But maintaining their crews posed a problem. Many crew members deserted once in California, to head for the gold fields. Some captains even resorted to holding their crew on board under guard while in port, or avoided San Francisco altogether. (The British would have the same problem later in Australia.)

The Civil War hampered American clipper-ship design and allowed Britain to catch up. By the mid-1860s, British clippers had become the fastest sailing ships in the world. Most were developed to compete in the lucrative tea run. The object was to be the first to transport a load of tea back to Britain in order to get the best price for the sponsor's cargo. One of the most famous races occurred when nine clipper ships left Foochow, China, in a race for London. After 99 days, two of the ships, *Ariel* and *Taeping*, docked in London within an hour of each other. Three other clipper ships docked within a day of the winner.

The Age of Steam

Few ships were more magnificent than the streamlined clippers, but the days of the clipper were very short. Ever-advancing *steamships* would soon take all the markets from the graceful clippers. The steamship *Charlotte Dundas* had been introduced as early as 1802, and Robert Fulton's *Clermont* was sailed on the Hudson River in 1807. These new ships signaled the way of the future. For the first time a power boat could ignore the fortunes of the wind. But sail-powered ships did not disappear overnight. Hedging their bets, ship designers for some time included both steam engines and sails in their creations.

The traditional occupations of the sea changed with the coming of the new steamships. The art of creating, maintaining, and flying sails was replaced by the tending of burning coal in huge boilers. The original use for fast steamships was as *mail packets*. A little later, steamships were used to ferry passengers short distances, such as across the English Channel. Later, the great steamship lines, such as the White Star Line and Cunard, commissioned large ships to be built for transatlantic crossings. The wealth of the United States and Britain made crossing the Atlantic most profitable. A tradition of accommodating first-class passengers in comfort and style was established.

The rise in immigration to the United States was another source of income for liner companies. Many *ocean liners* had a *steerage* class for immigrants. Steerage was a large, under-deck cargo hold, so named because it was near the ship's steering mechanism. All that generally was provided were tiers of bunks and a few cooking stoves; the passengers often had to bring their own food. Some ships were specially constructed to transport huge numbers of immigrants but, generally, older ships that had outlived the luxury routes were used. Conditions were appalling; luckily, however, crossings were now measured in weeks, rather than the months it had taken the old sailing vessels.

With the luxury ships, many service occupations that had long been associated with hotels—from *chambermaids* to *waiters*—appeared on board ship. Ultimately, the great passenger ships most closely resembled seagoing hotels and were staffed as such. Yet, the passenger ship had the added dimension of being an important transport vehicle. In World Wars I and II, these great ships were used to move troops and munitions. In World War II, the *Queen Mary* and *Queen Elizabeth* ferried thousands of soldiers across the Atlantic. As late as 1982, the *Queen Elizabeth II* was used in the Falklands War to take troops into the war zone.

The steamship also revolutionized the development of the cargo ship. By the late 19th century, both *refrigerated ships* to carry meat and primitive *oil tankers* were being

With the rise of immigration, crew and passengers were often checked by health officials, here in New York harbor, and sometimes held in quarantine. (By A. Berghaus, Harper's Weekly, October 8, 1887)

built. Today, oil tankers and *container ships* are vitally important to the survival of developed countries. Vast cargos can be transported very efficiently. The size of the ships has also increased greatly. These superships often reach over 1,000 feet and carry hundreds of thousands of tons of cargo. However, the age of automation has affected the numbers of the crew. These new giants generally carry a crew of less than 50 to care for the ship and manage the cargo. In the days of sail, the largest ships—about one-hundredth the size of today's superships—carried hundreds of sailors!

The development of steam also was important to the military, but it was just one of many 19th-century technological improvements that changed the face of naval warfare. During the early part of the century, wooden ships, like those commanded by Lord Nelson at Trafalgar in 1805, evolved into steel-hulled, powered craft with massive guns. The Battle of Trafalgar—with the British fleet facing a combined Franco-Spanish fleet—was one of the most decisive naval battles in history. The British Admiral Nelson, using revolutionary tactics, drove his fleet through the enemy formation and allowed his ships to close and destroy the French and Spanish vessels. The ships which fought this battle were the best of their time. They were wooden-hulled sailing vessels, which closely resembled ships that had been sailed hundreds of years earlier. But just a few decades later these ships were obsolete. Steam propulsion, more powerful naval ordnance, and armored ships created a whole new type of navy—a navy no longer dependent upon the wind, but on coal.

The battle between the *CSS Virginia* (also known as the *Merrimack*) and the *USS Monitor* during the American Civil War was a milestone in naval development. On March 6, 1862, the *Virginia* attempted to break a Union blockade. During the day, this remarkable armored steamship was able to sink several Union sailing ships—both with gunfire and by ramming. By nightfall, the Union ships had withdrawn out of range and the *Virginia* returned to its base. The next morning when the

Virginia sailed out to do battle with the Union fleet, it found its way opposed by the Union armored ship, the *Monitor*. The long battle between these two *ironclads* was indecisive tactically, but the *Monitor* won by default, since the blockade continued and the *Virginia* never challenged it again. With these new ships, fighting occupations evolved much as those on merchant ships. The main exception was that the battle stations demanded more, rather than fewer, crew.

During the late 19th and early 20th centuries an arms race was under way among nations such as Britain, the United States, France, Germany, and later, Japan. The aim was to build larger, more heavily armed and armored ships. This was the age of the *battleship*. In 1906, the British launched the *Dreadnought*. This made all existing battleships obsolete. The *Dreadnought* carried heavy-caliber guns, was constructed of thick armor, and was fitted with new turbine engines. All the other major countries copied the British design. Even so, by the start of World War I the British held a substantial superiority in number of capital ships—large warships such as battleships (and later aircraft carriers). The Germans exceeded the British ships in quality, however.

Throughout the war, the Germans made only one serious attempt to challenge the British command of the seas with surface ships. This was at the Battle of Jutland. During this battle, the Germans sank more ships than the British and killed more sailors. But Jutland remained a strategic victory for the British, since they forced the Germans to return to harbor, and the British continued to tie up the German fleet for the whole war. The battleship was supreme for a relatively brief time. Other ships, such as the fast *destroyers*, which carried torpedoes and mines, gradually became more important than battleships.

World War I also saw the first major use of a new vessel in war—the *submarine*—which the Germans used effectively. Undetectable, the submarine was able to sail past blockading ships and roam freely in the Atlantic. The German submarines sank a huge number of merchant ships carrying vital supplies to the British Isles. By 1917, the German submarines had brought the British to desperate straits. However, by using destroyers to convoy and protect merchant ships, the Allies eventually turned the tide. The submarine was the most effective naval weapon the Germans had in both world wars. It was a superb hunter of merchant ships, although indiscriminate sinking of unarmed ships angered neutral nations, such as the United States. The sinking of the passenger liner *Lusitania* helped turn the American public hard against Germany.

The submarine was an effective hunter, but was far from a pleasure to serve in. Cramped and even more starkly functional than surface ships, submarines packed crews in tightly—crews that were often subjected to the most horrifying type of attack. Submerged craft were attacked by surface vessels with *depth charges*. To many submariners, their ship must have appeared little more than a steel coffin as the explosions sounded nearby. And for many the submarine *was* a coffin. As soon as the Allies in both world wars produced effective counters, the German submarines became the hunted. Yet the submarine was and is a very important weapon. In both world wars, the German submarine force alone almost cut off supplies to the British. And during World War II,

Submarines were being caricatured for years before they developed as a practical working craft for naval use. ("Science Under Divers Forms," by George Cruikshank, 1843)

American submarines were responsible for almost two-thirds of the Japanese vessels destroyed. Today, the most advanced submarines are atomic-powered. Many carry nuclear ballistic missiles, which can strike an enemy thousands of miles away.

One other development in seapower changed the way sea battles were to be fought. This was the *aircraft carrier*. The ability to carry warplanes capable of bombing or torpedoing capital ships made the heavy battleship forces virtually obsolete. The aircraft carrier is essentially a sailing airfield. The crew includes *pilots* and other support personnel, in addition to sailors concerned with keeping the ship afloat. New skills had to be learned, as aircraft carriers came to dominate naval forces. Holding the ship steady in choppy seas so aircraft could be launched, and then determining how best to land planes on such a small surface, were crucial.

Modern fleets try to combine a variety of striking forces. Aircraft carriers are centers of strike forces surrounded by ships such as destroyers, *cruisers*, and *frigates* carrying ship-to-air missiles to guard against air attack. However, defending against "smart" missiles—those with their own internal guidance systems—launched miles from the target and skimming in over the surface of the ocean is not an easy task. Future developments are difficult to foretell.

Despite all this modern technology, however, at least one seagoing occupation continues as of old. Today parts of the Indian Ocean and the Caribbean are a new hotbed of pirates. Often engaged in drug running, modern pirates steal fast motor boats and use them to pick up their cargoes. The shallows, the thousands of small islands, and the skill of the runners make the area hard to police.

The sea has bred many specialists. But one deserves special mention: the *navigator* or *pilot*. From the earliest days of sailing, mariners desired to have among their crew at least one individual with special experience of the waters in which they were sailing. Since early sailors often followed the land, these navigators or pilots collected knowledge about the characteristics of the coastline—what landmarks dotted the route, where rocks and sandbars could be dangerous, where tides and whirlpools could threaten a ship, where pirates might lay in wait to attack ships, where the safe channels and good harbors lay, and other such vital information.

Later, when sailors began to cross the seas and oceans, they developed various other methods of navigation. Sometimes when crossing large bodies of water, they would release birds from their ships, much as Noah did from the ark; if the birds did not return, they would know they were near land. For many centuries, oceangoing sailors relied on the stars to guide them. In medieval times, India even had a special nautical school to train pilots in navigation by the stars. (*Caravan leaders* sometimes studied at the same schools, since they used the stars to guide them over the trackless desert.)

It is not surprising that when the first European sailors arrived in the East, they employed native pilots to help them. So when Portuguese sailor Vasco da Gama arrived in East Africa on the Indian Ocean in 1498, he engaged the great Indian pilot Ahmed ibn Majid, author of several standard books on navigation, to guide his ship safely to India. Later Europeans in Eastern waters sometimes used native pilots, but often relied on European sailors who had made previous voyages to the region. So it was that English navigator William Adams (inspiration for James Clavell's fictional hero in *Shogun*) arrived in Japan in the early 1600s as pilot for a Dutch ship.

In modern times, ship's navigators have had many technical aids to help them guide their ships safely to their destinations. The great Age of Discovery following da Gama's and Columbus's voyages resulted in the production of ever-better charts and maps. The use of devices like the quadrant and the compass helped navigators do their jobs more effectively, as do computers today.

Whatever navigational aids are used, however, pilots expert in local conditions have long been responsible for guiding a ship into harbor or through narrow waterways, such as rivers and canals. The distinct profession of *harbor pilot* dates back at least to Biblical times. The term "pilot" is a relatively modern one, however. It is believed to come from the Dutch words *pijl* and *lood*, or *pole-lead*, referring to the plumbs and sounding lines that early pilots used to measure the depth of the water as they proceeded. Today, of course, they use more sophisticated technical equipment, such as fathometers or computer sonar devices.

As other trades developed guilds, certainly by medieval times, so did pilots. The pilots' guild of England's port of Hull is said to have been founded in 1369. (Even in young America, the Sandy Hook pilots have been guiding ships into the port of New York since at least 1694.) These harbor pilots' guilds were—and are—self-perpetuating. The guild members decide on who should be admitted as apprentices; they oversee training, set pay rates and working hours, evaluate performance of guild members, and set aside common funds to aid pilots in need. Today, harbor pilots must also be licensed by the government to practice their trade. Openings are rare, and new harbor pilots are often relatives or friends of current guild members, or at least people who have considerable training and experience in local maritime conditions.

These harbor pilots are a very special breed. They train for many years—sometimes seven or more—studying in minute detail the harbor they serve, so that they can bring ships into it safely no matter what the weather. And they must serve at any time of the day or night, any time of the year, no matter what the weather, even in the worst gales.

Harbor pilots wait in a small pilot boat beyond the harbor mouth for the approach of a vessel. The pilot boat is brought alongside the large ship and the pilot climbs up the side on a ladder—itself no mean feat in the midst of a raging storm. Once aboard, the harbor pilot advises the ship's captain on the correct course until the ship is safely in its berth in the harbor. Then the pilot transfers to an outbound ship, guides it out of port, and is dropped back off at the pilot boat at sea.

In earlier times, pilots sometimes raced one another to get to a ship first, and so get the pilot's fee. Several pilots might race after one ship, leaving other ships to signal in vain for aid. On the other hand, harbor pilots were not always willing to go out to ships when the weather was bad. This was especially true in places where corruption had affected the pilotage system.

In early 19th-century New York, for example, some "political pilots"—often totally without experience—were granted licenses as favors. In stormy weather, ships sometimes frantically signaled for pilots off New York Harbor, while the "political pilots" played cribbage in a local tavern, warm and safe, refusing to venture out. The result could be tragic on occasion, as ships full of passengers foundered and sank outside the harbor mouth for lack of anyone to guide them safely in. Not surprisingly, such a situation was not allowed to last for long. The Sandy Hook Pilots Benevolent Association, working with the government, set modern standards and practices to ensure that only qualified mariners are appointed as pilots and that ships are served in an orderly and rational manner, in all weather.

The sea is bountiful in many ways. Millions of people make their living on the world's waterways. Few on Earth are untouched by produce transported by ship—and every seagoing power fully understands the importance of maintaining a navy to protect its trade routes. Although technology has evolved to aid them, today's sailors—among them some women, though still in small numbers—have much in common with those who worked the sea thousands of years ago. Whether or not they have computer assistance, sailors still must make all the decisions involved in sailing a ship safely. And they must carefully watch and prepare for any changes in the sea and the weather—both as dangerous then as now.

For related occupations in this volume, *Warriors and Adventurers*, see the following:

Flyers
Robbers and Other Criminals
Soldiers
Spies

For related occupations in other volumes of the series, see
the following:
in *Builders*:
Carpenters
Shipwrights
in *Communicators*:
Messengers and Couriers
in *Financiers and Traders*:
Merchants and Shopkeepers
in *Harvesters*:
Divers
Fishers
Whalers
in *Healers* (forthcoming):
Barbers
Physicians and Surgeons
in *Helpers and Aides*:
Drivers
Exterminators and Other Pest Controllers
in *Restaurateurs and Innkeepers* (forthcoming):
Innkeepers
in *Scientists and Technologists*:
Astronomers
Geographers
Mathematicians

Soldiers

The roots of military occupations stretch back into the darkness of prehistory. Archaeological excavations have uncovered a wide variety of weapons from sites all over the world. Crafted arrowheads and spearheads, bronze axes, and barbed bone clubs have all been found in abundance.

In early wars over land, hunting grounds, mates, and slaves, roving bands or individuals did the fighting, but as civilization developed, war became more complex. As people built cities and grouped together in large numbers, war became more than merely bands of disorganized warriors prowling the countryside, fighting with little order. At first, armies had no real specialization. Soldiers were often not a professional or even exclusive group. Even *cooks* in some armies were required to take up arms during emergencies.

Organized warfare developed as civilizations emerged from the fertile lands in the Middle East and China. Among the earliest and greatest of the kingdoms that rose, flourished, and fell in those times was Egypt. At first Egyptian armies were little more than unorganized bands of recruits, with levies being called up to attack and repel invaders. A *levy* was something like the modern draft, but far less formal. As the kingdom prospered, Egypt became one of the first civilizations to be able to afford a standing army, composed of *infantry* (foot soldiers) armed with bronze swords, as well as supporting troops such as *archers* and *slingers*.

A major event occurred in about 1800 B.C. that had a great effect upon Egyptian military organization: The country was invaded by the Hyksos, a nomadic, Semitic people probably from Palestine. The Hyksos used the horse and *chariot* to sweep through Egypt, conquering

In this assault of a fort, soldiers are employing the testudo *and scaling ladders. (From* History of Egypt, *by Clara Erskine Clement, 1901)*

Early soldiers were often essentially marines, transported to the battle site by water, as on this Nile boat c. 2500 B.C. (By Manning de V. Lee, from Historic Ships, *by Rupert Sargent Holland, 1926)*

the entire country by 1700 B.C., and holding sway over the native populace for another hundred years. When the Hyksos were finally driven out, the Egyptians adapted the chariot for their own use. It became a vitally important military vehicle throughout the Middle East, providing troops with a previously unheard-of mobility. The light chariot usually held a *driver* (the *charioteer*), an archer, and a *shield-bearer*. The driver of the chariot was trained to maneuver the vehicle along the flanks of the opposing force, probing for any exploitable weaknesses, while the archer harassed the enemy with arrows. When the enemy lines broke, the chariot could also be used to pursue and destroy the retreating army. Military use of the chariot laid the base for Egyptian power, which grew through the 15th century B.C. and at its height extended from modern Libya all the way through Palestine and Syria, right to the edge of the Hittite Empire in what is now Turkey.

Alongside Egypt other kingdoms developed in the Middle East: Sumer, Akkad, Phoenicia, the Hittites, Babylonia. The soldiers in their armies were both levies and *mercenaries*, who made a profession of fighting for whoever paid them. They fought as infantry and with chariots. Phoenicia especially developed a powerful navy to protect its wide-ranging merchant trade, which crisscrossed the Mediterranean. Phoenician soldiers were often transported to battle sites around the sea by ship, at times doubling as sailors.

Sometime during the 13th century B.C., an important technological advance revolutionized warfare: the discovery and use of *iron*. Thought to have been first used by the Hittites, iron weapons had a tremendous impact on warfare. Much stronger and less brittle than copper and bronze, iron was soon in use in most of the local armies. Of the great military powers in the Middle East, the one to use the new, more efficient iron weapons most effectively was Assyria. For almost five centuries, from the twelfth to the seventh century B.C., Assyria was the major power in the area. There are several reasons for Assyria's success. Not only did it make many technical improvements in the iron weapons, but it also developed a more efficient organization. Assyria was a heavily militaristic society ruled by a *king* who had extensive military training and experience. The army itself was composed of highly organized infantry, charioteers, archers, and *cavalry*, troops mounted on horses, or sometimes camels. No other army at the time could match them.

Assyria had another extremely effective weapon in its arsenal: terror. Assyrian victories were accompanied by orgies of bloodshed. The Assyrians demanded surrender; if a city resisted surrender and later fell, the Assyrians had all the inhabitants put to the sword, impaled, flayed, or burned alive. Fear of the Assyrian terror tactics was often enough to bring about the immediate surrender of a besieged city. Little wonder that when previous victims of the Assyrian atrocities—specifically the Babylonians and Medes—finally toppled the Assyrian Empire, they meted out brutality in kind.

The soldiers of this era—whether in the Middle East, India, or China—generally fought in relatively unorganized groups. The major weapons were the *spear*, the *javelin*, the *bow*, the *sling*, and the *sword*. Chariots appeared in about 1800 B.C. and cavalry was in use by 1000 B.C. A typical battle would begin with an exchange

of missile weapons—arrows, rocks, and javelins—and then the infantry would close, stabbing and hacking at each other until one side broke. Finally, the chariots and cavalry would harass the defeated enemy, sometimes causing a disorderly retreat.

The growth of towns lead to new concepts in warfare—the twin sciences of *fortification* and *siegecraft*—that have mirrored each other through the ages. As defenses became stronger, the machines and techniques used to besiege fortifications became more effective. Throughout history, one art would dominate the other, but never for too long. Many of the early cities were walled to keep out the various nomadic invaders. We are all familiar with the Biblical story of the fall of Jericho, an early and highly successful siege, but the people who first refined siegecraft and fortification to the point of science were the Assyrians. Their walled cities

Assyrian soldiers excelled at warfare using chariots like these, from the seventh century B.C. (Louvre)

and methods of assault awed their neighbors. Their cities were impregnable for centuries, while their machines of war forced the capitulation of many strong towns and cities.

The primary weapon of this age was the spear. The men who carried polearms formed the heart of most early armies, for a group of well-trained soldiers wielding spears was formidable. The weapon was fairly simple—a long, straight wooden pole tipped with metal. At a stage when many societies could not produce much metal, the spear usually could be made easily in large quantities, since it was relatively inexpensive. Several spearheads could be constructed for every sword. In fact, generally only individuals with money and rank could afford a costly iron sword. Many of the warriors of this age had to provide their own arms; the military leaders in each country dictated exactly what type of weapon a person of a specific rank should have.

The spear was an excellent weapon; long, heavy spears could hold the enemy away, while lighter spears could be thrown at an enemy while still at a distance. Simple in construction, the spear was far from simple to use. The best *spearmen* had one thing in common: rock-hard discipline. To face another large body of spearmen—or contingents of cavalry, archers, and slingers who could pour in missile fire from a distance—demanded a strict formation in which individual soldiers could trust their partners.

The Greeks

The Greeks were the first of the super spearmen. Like other early soldiers, the free Greek citizens had to provide their own armor, spear, and sword. Refining a formation used by Egyptians, Babylonians, and Assyrians, they turned the *phalanx* into the most successful formation of its day. Although it underwent several modifications, the basic Greek phalanx can best be described as a rectangle composed of eight to twelve lines of spearmen. The Greeks would form in a series of escalating groups—*platoons, companies*, and *battalions*—with the ultimate end of creating the phalanx. Once in formation, the soldiers would steadily advance toward the enemy, eight-foot-long spears lowered and pointing outwards. When closing with an enemy, the soldiers would break into a run, if the ground was flat enough, so they would not be forced to break their formation. The first two ranks would engage the enemy directly, while the rear ranks added force and supplied replacements for the fallen in the first ranks. The Greek phalanx was stiff and inflexible, but absolutely nothing in existence at the time could face it. The hardy, independent Greeks who formed the phalanx

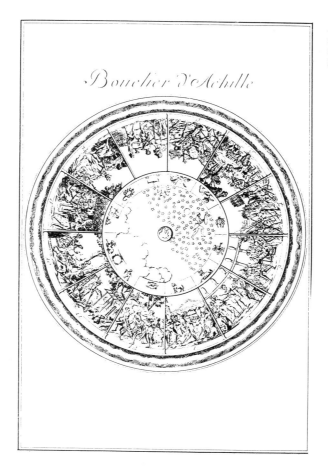

Achilles' shield includes scenes of the great Greek soldiers in battle. (From Diderot's Encyclopedia, *late 18th century)*

were heavily armored with *breastplates, greaves* (a type of armor to protect the soldier's legs), *helmets*, and *shields*.

The Greeks' culture and ideals also contributed to their military success. The Greeks constantly trained as *athletes*; the development of the body was as important as that of the mind, and Greek soldiers were generally in top physical condition. Skills were also honed for the great all-Greek contest, the *Olympics*, held every four years. Originally designed to further the arts of war, these contests stressed running for endurance, javelin-throwing, boxing, and wrestling. The games also served another purpose—to give the Greeks a strong identity as Greeks. Although they constantly fought and bickered among themselves, the Greeks were able to recognize their kinship and ally themselves against outside threats.

The most effective armies included a variety of different troops in their ranks. They tried to find the best mix of missile soldiers, light infantry (archers and slingers), heavy infantry shock forces, and cavalry. Troops that were strong in one category and weak in another often suffered severely unless the commander chose the battle site and time carefully. The Greek armies included a number of light infantry missile troops that skirmished outside the phalanx, but they generally depended upon their magnificent heavy infantry, the *hoplites*. When these soldiers, who were primarily spearmen, were able to meet their enemies on favorable ground, they often defeated them handily. Some of these soldiers were specially armed and trained essentially as *marines*, who were transported by ship to places of battle or whose fighting came in connection with sea campaigns, as was common for the seagoing Greeks. Marines have formed a specialty within soldiering for centuries, right up to today.

The first severe test of Greek arms occurred during the Greco-Persian Wars that took place during the fifth century B.C. The Persian armies had been highly successful elsewhere. Successors of the Assyrians, Babylonians, and Medes, they had carved out an empire that covered most of western Asia—a vast territory with dozens of different cultures. The Persian army was a force dependent upon levied troops and mercenaries from many regions, especially lightly armored archers and cavalry. Most of its infantry was also lightly armored, although there was a force of respected infantry known as the "Immortals," who served as the emperor's bodyguard. However, most of the Persians' subject forces had little thought about the greater glory of the Persian Empire. They were neither well-trained nor well-regarded by the commanders. So, although the Persian army vastly outnumbered the Greek army, its true superiority was not as great as supposed.

The Persians' first setback came when they invaded Greece. At the Battle of Marathon, 20,000 Persians under the command of Emperor Darius faced about 10,000 Athenians and Plateans, most of them hoplites. In the ensuing battle the Greeks actually surrounded the more numerous Persian force and forced them to retreat, winning a decisive victory. The Persians were far from finished with Greece, however. Darius planned his revenge, but died before he could put another invasion into effect. His successor, Xerxes, continued with the plan to subjugate Greece, gathering an enormous army—some sources claim up to 200,000 men. But he failed. The Persian superiority in numbers was totally offset by the better-disciplined, better-armed, better-motivated Greeks and their phalanx. First at the naval Battle of Salamis and later at the Battle of Platea, the Greeks proved the Persians were no match for them. The Greek city-states kept their freedom and defeated the mightiest empire of the time.

The next century was filled with the exploits of the Greek infantry. One example of the Greek infantry's extraordinary strength is the March of the Ten Thousand. At the beginning of the fourth century B.C., Cyrus, the Persian governor of Lydia, sought to take the crown from his brother, Artaxerxes II. The cream of Cyrus's army was a force of 10,000 Greek mercenaries. Cyrus took his army into the heart of the Persian Empire and engaged his brother at the Battle of Cunaxa, where the Greeks routed the army of Artaxerxes almost on their own. Unfortunately for them, Cyrus was killed and his Persian troops fled, leaving the Greeks stranded.

Suddenly, the Greek force found itself somewhere in western Asia, over 1,000 miles from the sea. The Persian emperor first invited all the commanders of the Greeks to a feast, pretending to parley. Instead, he treacherously had them murdered. He reasoned that, leaderless, the Greek troops would panic and disintegrate as a fighting unit. They did not. On the contrary, they elected new officers and, under the leadership of a noble named Xenophon, they marched homeward. It took over five months of trekking, fighting almost every step of the way, but they finally reached the sea and safety. More than 6,000 Greeks survived. On their way to safety, they had fought every force the Persian Empire could bring against them. The lesson was not lost. Less than a century later, Alexander the Great would lead his army back to Persia and quickly conquer it with the same type of soldier who had served under Xenophon.

Alexander the Great and his father, Philip II of Macedon, introduced a variety of new elements to warfare. From a comparatively backward kingdom, Philip II fought with success against northern barbarian tribes and then turned his attention southward to the Greek city-states. He soon conquered all of Greece, defeating a combined Greek force of 50,000 at the Battle of Chaeronea in 338 B.C.

The army Philip used evolved out of the Greek model. The phalanx was still the basic unit, but it had been developed to become a much more maneuverable formation. In the Macedonian phalanx, the duties of the Greek hoplites were divided between two types of soldiers: the *pezetaeri* and the *hypaspists*. The *pezetaeri* carried lengthened pikes (*sarissas*), which were up to 18 feet long. The *hypaspists* fought as a single force in small-scale actions and as adjuncts to the *pezetaeri* in larger battles. They had the ability to move quickly and meet any threat from flank attacks. They could also hold off any enemy, covering for the slower movements of the *pezetaeri*, who had the disadvantage of having to turn their longer weapons.

Under first Philip and then Alexander, the science of combining the various arms of the military progressed. Although the phalanx was the heart of the force, the Macedonians also had strong cavalry, missile, and artillery units. The cavalry was actually the elite force, composed of skilled horsemen from the best Macedonian families. Archers and slingers maintained a harassing fire against the enemy, while the infantry and cavalry moved in unison. In addition, the Macedonians introduced several new variations in field artillery, notably in *catapults*, slingshot-type machines for launching objects called *missiles*, and *ballistae*, bow-type machines for propelling missiles.

The Macedonians were particularly skillful in siegecraft. Philip and Alexander both made extensive use of the most skilled *engineers* of their time. Macedonian armies included a corps of engineers, who could be counted upon to construct engines of war, bridges, or earthworks. When Alexander laid siege to Tyre, he had his engineers build a mole (an earthen causeway) from the mainland to the island city. This was no easy task, since the city was nearly half a mile from the mainland and very well defended. Alexander's engineers solved the problem, however. They not only created the mole, but they also devised a way to breach the city walls from the seaboard side, using ships.

City defenders had their champions, too. Perhaps the most famous was the great Greek *scientist* Archimedes. Archimedes was one of the most talented men of his or any other age. He is famous for the "Eureka!" incident, in which he is said to have run into the street naked shouting *eureka* ("I have found [it]") after discovering the principle of displacement of water in his tub. He also developed the laws of the lever and balance. He is quoted as saying that, given a place to stand and a fixed fulcrum, he could move the Earth. Archimedes constructed a number of intricate machines that could move heavy loads.

It was a short step to creating machines of war. King Hieron, delighted with Archimedes' work, asked him to invent new weapons for the city of Syracuse. He happily went to work and developed quite a few. After King Hieron died, Syracuse became involved in a war with nearby Rome, ultimate successor to much of the empire Alexander had carved. Archimedes was about 75 at the time, but he took charge of the defense of the city. The Romans had expected an easy victory and attacked simultaneously with an army and a navy. Archimedes's inventions gave them a nasty surprise. The Romans were subjected to a seemingly never-ending torrent of projectiles, which stopped their attacks dead. There are no accurate records of what Archimedes' weapons were. Speculation ranges from fine improvements on existing weapons to totally new concepts. One interesting weapon Archimedes was supposed to have constructed was a type of super magnifying glass, which could set the Roman ships on fire if they ventured too close to the city walls.

In the end, Syracuse fell after a siege of about eight months. The Romans were led by a tough, resourceful officer, Marcellus, who, though impressed with Archimedes's weapons, knew he could capture the city eventually. The Romans at last got into the city using an age-old method: guile. They made a surprise attack during a festival. Marcellus gave strict orders that Archimedes not be harmed. A Roman soldier discovered him working on some mathematical problems and ordered the old scientist to follow him to Marcellus. Archimedes declined, saying that he wanted to finish the problem he was working on. Not used to being challenged, the soldier out of hand slew the greatest mind of the age.

The example of Archimedes is not unique in the history of warfare. Quite often mathematical and scientific geniuses bent their minds to the problems of warfare. Countries with a strong scientific intellectual class often used these special citizens' talents. *Weaponmakers* for centuries worked as auxiliaries to the various military occupations, and many early scientists considered creating weapons of war as an interesting sideline—at least until the age of technology was ushered in with the Industrial Revolution.

Macedonian leaders made effective use of such technological innovations. Philip of Macedon also created a superb logistical and medical apparatus for his troops. He took advantage of Greek skills in medicine and engineering. Highly regarded *surgeons* and engineers accompanied his armies, a practice which the Romans later followed. Together, training, supply, and care helped make the Macedonian army one of the most successful military forces in history. With this army, Alexander conquered most of the known world, from Egypt to India.

The Romans

The Macedonian phalanx and the glories of Alexander's conquests were later eclipsed by perhaps the most successful military organization of all time: the Roman *legion*. The success of Rome was remarkable: one small city-state on the Italian peninsula came to control, politically or economically, most of Europe, North Africa, and the Middle East. But, impressive as it may have been, this control was not due to inherent Roman superiority in culture, law, or administration. It was due to the great efficiency of the Roman army.

The early history of the Roman Republic is a tale of creeping Roman expansionism throughout the Italian peninsula. Roman arms defeated neighboring cities, and Roman organization welded them into participating members of Roman society. During its first few centuries of existence, the Roman military force was similar in recruitment to that of the Greek city-states. Free citizens were called up and formed into *militias*. As in the Greek armies, the recruits were well-trained, highly motivated soldiers who could be considered almost professional.

Many historians link the success of the Roman army to the zeal of the free Romans who made up the ranks. This may be true, in part, but the greater factor was the unified approach of the Roman army. Soldiers were not only well-trained but also well-led and able to function in well-ordered formations, which could overwhelm the masses of disorganized "barbarians" who often opposed them. Indeed, the two times they met, the Romans soundly defeated the Macedonian phalanx as well.

The Roman army combined all the elements of warfare: light infantry, heavy infantry, cavalry, and missile troops, both archers and slingers. Like the Greeks, the Romans paid most attention to their heavy infantry. It was the backbone of the force. The *legionnaires* in it were armed with the famous Roman short sword, the *gladius*, and a javelin known as a *pilium*. The archers and slingers were primarily mercenaries.

The Roman formation was quite different from the Greek and Macedonian phalanxes. The phalanx had been primarily a closed formation, with lines of troops attacking and defending shoulder-to-shoulder behind an array of pikes, sticking out like the needles of a hedgehog. The Roman legion's lines were more fluid. The original legion was composed of many *maniples*, small units of 160 men. Within the maniples, each infantryman was given about five square yards—enough room to swing and thrust effectively with his sword. The Roman line also presented a very flexible front to the enemy. If pressed hard, the first line could fall back into the second line. Also the *pilia* (javelins) were used with great effect as missile weapons, either to stop an attacking enemy or prepare for a charge.

The Roman legion adapted with the change that came to Rome itself. As the republic developed into an empire, the army evolved from a part-time militia of citizen-soldiers into a standing force. The far-flung outposts of an empire that stretched from Palestine to Britain demanded a large number of units to patrol and protect Roman trading interests. The army underwent a major transformation. Legionnaires began to be recruited from all levels of society, not just the highest. (Slaves, non-Romans, and lower-class Romans had, before then, largely been confined to auxiliary units.) The army also came to be looked upon as a career by more and more people in the society. The Roman leaders were equal to the task of reorganization. In essence, they forged a professional army whose scope and mission approach those of modern forces.

As any new American recruit in the army or marines quickly learns, training and discipline are favored tools for creating a solid, coordinated unit. The Romans developed a system for training and maintaining a professional army—one that protected a huge empire for more than 300 years. Basic training in the modern armed services is similar to that which the Roman legionnaires received.

Recruits were forced to learn to march in unison with their unit. In battle, ranks had to be maintained, and the Romans often won because of their iron discipline in the face of overwhelming odds. Throughout the history of both the republic and the empire there are examples of Roman armies defeating opposing forces ten times and more their size. From the beginning, recruits forcibly learned that they were cogs in a greater whole. They learned how to quickly respond to superiors and how to mesh with their fellow troops. Part and parcel with marching was physical training. Recruits were put through the paces in running, swimming, and jumping. The training began without full arms and then progressed until the recruits could perform in full battle dress.

Next came weapons training. In addition to the *gladius*, Roman soldiers carried large, rectangular shields for protection. To reach a high level of proficiency with weapons, the recruits trained with practice swords and shields that were twice as heavy as the real weapons. Wooden stakes set in the ground were very important in the training process. Many Roman commanders stressed practice with the stakes as the best way to teach soldiers the rudimentaries that would sustain them in battle—much as a modern trainer stresses target practice. These stakes were treated seriously as opponents. Recruits struck pretend blows, gave way and attacked the various parts of the stake representing head, torso, and legs. The Romans stressed using the point of the sword. Roman troops often faced opponents skilled in the use of the edge of the sword who were able to slash at their enemies with a great deal of vigor. However, a slashing attack often left the swordsman open to a strong counter thrust—and Roman training emphasized taking advantage of this weakness.

After graduating from the first level, recruits would be given real weapons for practice. They must have seemed wonderfully light and manageable in comparison to the heavy wooden practice weapons. The final stage in training was setting two recruits in combat with one another. The fights were as brutal and realistic as possible, but the weapons were blunted and had wooden buttons to reduce injury.

The sword was the most important weapon of the

The chaos of battle is well depicted in this second century A.D. sculpture. (Museo Nazionale delle Terme, Rome)

legionnaire, but Roman soldiers were versatile fighters who learned the use of several weapons, among them the *pilium*. A practice *pilium*, twice as heavy as the real weapon, was employed. The theory was that practicing with the heavier weapon would strengthen the throwing arm. The *pilium* in battle was most often used as a throwing weapon. Infantrymen generally carried two. As the enemy came within range, a volley of these spears would shower down upon them. The heads of the *pilia* were designed so that they would either bend or break off. This served two purposes. First, the spears would be useless to the enemy, so they could not turn them against their owners. Second, if the *pilium* lodged in a shield, armor, or flesh, it would tend to drag down whatever it struck. A shield with one or two of these weapons stuck in it would be hard to hold up; once it was lowered, the owner would be an easy target.

Some Romans were taught the use of the *bow*. They, like modern *sharpshooters*, would set up targets at various distances to get the feel of range. Similarly, certain troops were trained in the use of the *sling*. This simple but effective weapon was merely two leather thongs attached to a pocket of leather. The stone or lead missile was placed in the pocket and then the sling was swung about the head, one thong was released, and the missile flew out with great velocity. Although simple, this weapon demanded skill and practice. Most of the slingers in the Roman army were mercenaries recruited as light troops. In addition, all soldiers were required to learn how to throw stones. At close quarters, and with no other weapon handy, stones would serve a last-ditch purpose.

After basic training, the soldiers were further trained in the field. They learned the art of war firsthand—which for them, at this stage, consisted mainly of carrying heavy loads long distances and then preparing and digging fortifications. Like soldiers of today, Roman recruits were kept very busy with an endless variety of tasks. Most of the time, the Roman soldiers were not fighting. During the quiet periods, they were contracted out as *laborers* or were engaged in construction projects for the good of the empire, notably roadbuilding. The army officers would also serve as a type of *police* force during periods of extended peace. At the end of the training period, the recruits would take their places among the other soldiers in their legion. The army's success was partly due to the Roman genius for organization and supply. The entire Roman Empire was a remarkably well-governed area. It was kept united with no modern communication technology; weeks or even months could pass before orders from Rome could arrive at outposts.

The Romans also were no strangers to siegecraft and fortification. Their engineers were probably the best trained in the world at the time and followed the legions in their conquests. On campaigns, the Romans would take tools and equipment that would help them construct war machines in the field. The engineers were also skilled in constructing bridges and earthworks. The Romans invented the concept of *field fortification*. To make an army of conquest secure in hostile territory, the engineers would direct the construction of a *castrametation*. This was a fortified camp and could be quickly and easily set up each night, if need be. The Romans, as usual, were very well organized. Each soldier was assigned a specific task. In short order, a ditch would be dug and a defensive palisade of sharpened stakes would be thrown up around the camp.

There has been some argument about the purpose and construction of early Roman artillery weapons, but they can basically be classified by purpose and method of propulsion. All were designed to hurl some sort of projectile, but used one of two methods of propulsion: *torsion* and *tension*. Torsion was the twisting of some fibrous material—twine, rope, or, on occasion, human hair—around a shaft. The skein was twisted very tightly; then the shaft, bent back and locked in place, could accept some type of missile, generally a large stone. When fired, the staff would spring forward, usually stopped by a strong wooden crossbar, while the missile continued on its path toward the target. This type of weapon was the basic catapult. It was also known by many other names; for example, the Romans called it an *onager*, their word for a mule or ass, because of the way it lurched and kicked.

Tension is the more familiar method of bending a wooden or steel bow. Here, the power was not in the twisted cord, but rather in the strength of the bow. Machines resembling huge crossbows could fire a variety of projectiles, from stones to javelin-sized missiles. They could be used to batter fortifications or to attack the enemy directly. They were also known by several names, which can be lumped under the term *ballistae*. Although most ballistae were tension-powered, there were some exceptions. Torsion-powered ballistae had twin bows powered by the cords wrapped around them.

For their time, these engines of war were very effective. The operators were highly skilled people who knew these machines inside and out, since they had to construct them right in the field. They also were familiar with the rudiments of elevation, aiming, twisting cords, and assessing wind speed and direction. Depending upon the size and power of the machine, the strongest could toss a 50-100 pound stone several hundred yards with great force and some accuracy. Stones were not the only projectiles used. A particularly gruesome practice was to shoot the heads of captured enemies into besieged towns to induce them to surrender—an early form of psychological warfare. An early type of germ warfare was also practiced. Rotting parts of animals and carts of manure would also be fired into a besieged town in hopes that disease would spread. Some ballistae could be impressively powerful. There are accounts of bolts fired by these machines stabbing right through armored soldiers.

Yet for all their power, these war engines were not able to batter down the thick walls of well-built fortifications or major cities. The besieger had to resort to several other tricks and techniques to capture a resolutely defended town or fort. In many cases, several methods had to be used in concert for an assault to be successful.

A typical siege would often begin with the stronger enemy force encamping near the object of their siege. Archers, slingers, and war machines on both sides would try to maintain a deadly rain. The attacking army would initially probe to test the enemy's defenses. A contingent of soldiers might race ahead with a battering ram to try to breach the gate. In response, the defenders on the wall would try to repulse the attack, killing the assaulting force and capturing or crushing the ram.

Typically, the attacking force's initial assault would fail. At this stage, if they had the time and means, the attackers would try to starve the defending garrison into submission. If the cordon of soldiers surrounding the wall was not tight enough, the siege could literally last for years. During this war of attrition—gradually wearing down the enemy—the attackers and defenders were not totally idle. The attackers would often try to dig a mine under the walls of the city or fort and collapse a section for an assault to be conducted through. If the defenders discovered the mine, they would sink a countermine in response. When the two shafts met, there would be a brutal struggle, often in pitch blackness. If the mine were undiscovered, a section of the wall could be destroyed by undermining the foundation. When the breach appeared, the attackers would quickly try to storm that position, overwhelming the defenders before they could repair the damage. The defenders would try to hold out as long as possible. Often, well-constructed ancient cities had a strong, central defensive area. In the siege of Syracuse, defenders in the inner town were able to hold out for several months before the Romans prevailed.

The Roman Empire and its military arm, the legion, set a standard that almost all other countries since have striven to match. In fact, the Roman army was a well-oiled machine that had many elements common to the modern armies of today. In addition to fighting soldiers, it included a number of other specialists. Engineers built the military roads, siege equipment, and camps. *Messengers* efficiently linked the vast reaches of the

Roman Empire and the distant outposts and armies. *Scouts* gathered information for field armies. *Quartermasters* kept the forces armed, fed, and clothed. And surgeons cared for the troops. The organization worked very well—and it was not until modern times that any armed force could match the Roman army in depth or skill in support.

But the Roman Empire did finally collapse. Its foes were becoming more numerous and much more clever. Tactics were evolving. The actual composition of the Roman forces was, some claimed, deteriorating in quality. Too many non-Romans were allowed to enter the army—long gone were the sturdy civilian troops who had formed the heart of the army. In addition, the tribes and countries Rome held at bay were now much more familiar with the methods used by the Romans.

The Romans, to their credit, attempted to change themselves. The Battle of Adrianople in the fourth century A.D. was the primary catalyst. In this battle, Gothic horsemen annihilated a Roman army under the command of Valens, the Eastern Roman emperor. (By this time the empire had split into two separately administered divisions, the Western Empire ruled from Rome and the Eastern Empire ruled from Constantinople.) This battle essentially put an end to the legion as the dominant fighting force of the time. The Romans tried to adapt by developing their cavalry.

Infantry, for the most part, took a back seat to cavalry throughout much of the world at this time. Different types of horsemen had developed, among them the heavily armed Germanic cavalry and the very swift, more mobile cavalry of the Huns and other Eastern peoples. The light cavalry depended upon rushes around the fringes of the enemy army, firing arrows at a distance and severely weakening an enemy before attempting to close. The heavy cavalry of the German tribes was better able to close with the enemy using shock tactics.

Asian Warriors

Contemporary with the Roman Empire, the Chinese Empire, under the great Han dynasty, was developing its own superb army. China had had an effective chariot fighting force in earlier times, but in this period it sent an army halfway across Asia—following a route that would become the great Silk Road—bringing back large, powerful horses to replace their smaller ponies. As would be expected in a country famed for its central administration, the Chinese army was administered by professionals, many of them staff members in the imperial government. The empire was divided into territories, each of which was assigned a commander. As in many other countries in early times, the leaders and many of the soldiers were initially drawn from the elite classes. But later the Chinese began to draw on a wider variety of people for the army, among them political dissidents (who were sent to man border posts, far from their power bases) and petty criminals.

This was especially true when the Chinese turned toward defense, building the first of many versions of their Great Wall. Like soldiers elsewhere, the Chinese defensive troops were initially put to work building the fortification itself. Watchtowers were built first, it seems, so lookouts could spot attacking forces and alert the laboring soldiers to return to the structures' defensive positions. Later, after the wall was completed, the lookouts were kept on duty to watch the horizon, as China's early warning system. To protect its trade routes westward across Asia, the Chinese also built a series of forts along the old Silk Road, where soldiers both provided defense and tilled the land, thus supplying protection and fresh food for people traveling through the vast wastelands controlled by China.

These defensive measures were made necessary by the existence of an exceptionally powerful fighting force in the heart of Eurasia. There, on the great steppes, nomadic tribes of varied ethnic backgrounds had developed the skill of riding horses. By the eighth century B.C. the mounted archer had come onto the scene, threatening the settled nations all around Asia, in

In early India, soldiers made up a prominent and distinct warrior caste. (From History of India, *by Fannie Roper Feudge, 1903)*

China, India, the Near East, and Europe. The archers developed a devastating maneuver called the *Parthian shot*, often today called the *parting shot*. It involved a force of mounted archers apparently retreating and then suddenly wheeling on their relaxed enemies with a series of shots fired over their shoulders. With their great speed, their ability to wheel and turn sharply, and their ease at surrounding less mobile chariots, this cavalry struck terror into the settled civilizations—and ended the chariot as a true fighting weapon. These steppe cavalry did not develop the techniques of siegecraft, so the defensive walls and structures had some effect at keeping them out. But on their home ground, they were virtually unbeatable, and in many periods in history, they would—for a variety of reasons, among them in-

Central Asian archers were more often seen rapidly wheeling on horseback than in this rather static pose. (From The New America and the Far East, *1901)*

creased population or drought—explode outward from the steppe, attacking the urban lands on Asia's rim.

From these lands came the attackers who finally broke the power of Rome in Western Europe. During the fifth and sixth centuries, the Western Roman Empire was at last destroyed by the weight of several invasions from the steppe. First Attila and his Huns swept through both Eastern and Western empires. He was finally halted in Gaul (modern France) by a combined German-Roman force at the Battle of Chalons. After Attila's death, the huge Hunnish Empire broke apart. Vassal German tribes claimed what was once Roman territory for themselves.

Although the Western Empire died, Roman traditions—altered to suit a curious geographical and philosophical position between East and West—lived on in the Eastern Empire, which was better known as the Byzantine Empire. This empire would last for another thousand years after Rome's fall. In the Byzantine Empire, warfare was as carefully studied as it had been in Rome. The most important type of soldier in the Byzantine army was the *cataphract*, a horseman who was heavily armored, but who could also shoot a bow from horseback. In a sense, this horseman was a combination of the best of East and West. Well trained and led, the Byzantine cavalry helped keep at bay the wild, mobile Asiatic tribes. The *cataphract* was more heavily armored and able to charge through the lighter Eastern cavalry, while still able to avoid the flowing traps and envelopments that would later prove disastrous to the Western cavalry during the Crusades.

The Byzantines left two military treatises which illustrate the basic philosophy of the empire. The works, *Strategikon* and *Tactica*, are separated by several centuries in time, but they both show the genius the Byzantines had for sizing up an enemy and developing a method for dealing with a threat. The Byzantines never lacked enemies. The rise of Islam, which swiftly fanned out into Asia, severely buffeted the Byzantine Empire. Several Moslem peoples emerged to challenge the

Byzantines and attempt to conquer parts of the Empire. Essentially, as the treatises point out, the Byzantine strategy was to fight defensively. They had no desire to conquer more territory, since during its height, the empire encompassed much of the Middle East, Thrace, the Anatolian provinces, and many Mediterranean islands.

Like the Romans, the Byzantines relied upon a standing army, which was recruited from among the most warlike citizens of the empire. Although the armored *cataphracts* were the most important soldiers, the Byzantines did not ignore the other arms. The Byzantine infantry, *scutai*, was well trained and used in combination with the cavalry. The Byzantines also maintained a large navy, which kept the Mediterranean open for many years.

Byzantine technology was so advanced it created a weapon that, in itself, helped keep Constantinople's thick walls free of enemies for many hundreds of years. This was *Greek fire*, a secret, copper-based chemical composition which is unknown to modern science. It would burst into flames when wet and was extremely difficult to extinguish. This powerful weapon kept enemies in terror and was particularly effective in naval battles.

Another notable element of the Byzantine military were the mercenaries, probably the most famous being the elite Varangian Guard. The guard was composed principally of Scandinavian troops who were famous for their fearlessness. Harold Hardradda, known as last of the Vikings, was a commander of the guard. Later, when he was king of Norway, he invaded Anglo-Saxon England and was killed by Harold of Wessex at the Battle of Stamford Bridge. This distraction allowed William the Conqueror to land unopposed and later defeat the English at the Battle of Hastings. After the Norman Conquest, some exiled English warriors joined the Varangian Guard. In Eastern Europe, Constantinople (Byzantium) stood as a bulwark against the Asiatic tribes.

Soldiers in the Middle Ages

By the sixth century A.D., Western Europe had been thrown into chaos, as many Germanic tribes vied with one another for Roman lands. As Rome collapsed, Germanic invasions also took place in Britain, Gaul, Spain, Italy, and North Africa. The invaders carved out kingdoms, some of which lasted a few years before disintegrating, while others lasted centuries. Two of the most successful kingdoms were those in Britain and Gaul.

In Britain, the Angles, Saxons, and Jutes were invaders originally brought in to help the native British fight the ravaging Picts and Scots. These mercenaries soon turned the tables on their employers and conquered Britain. It was not a swift conquest; it took more than 100 years. The Anglo-Saxons suffered many reverses at the hands of the British Celts, and they also had to fight the Scots and Picts. Indeed, the legend of King Arthur is probably based upon some historic leader who unified the British kingdoms and heavily defeated the Anglo-Saxons at the Battle of Mount Badon. One theory is that the British resurrected old Roman military tactics and organization to push back the less sophisticated invaders. But it was a transitory victory and, in the end, the British were hemmed into the two Cymric kingdoms of Wales and Strathclyde.

The soldiers who fought at this time in Britain were mainly rather undisciplined infantry. Some of the British may have remembered Roman tactics, but they were ultimately unsuccessful. The Anglo-Saxons and Jutes also were not professional soldiers, but rather were invaders who sought to capture homesteads and start families. These types of soldiers were typical throughout this period and for many hundreds of years to follow. The vast majority of soldiers were not professionals in the strictest sense. They did, however, live and breathe conflict. Weapons of war were as natural to them as farming implements.

Therefore, the invaders often had an advantage.

Forceful leaders were able, by their own personal prestige, to weld together a group of fighters. The people invaded then tried to mobilize to repel the invaders. Since they, too, lacked true professionals, gathering their scattered forces took time and was often ineffectual. Only as kingdoms became stronger and more centralized did the invaded areas begin to offer more resistance. During the reigns of particularly strong sovereigns, such as Charlemagne and Alfred, organized forces became far more effective.

The weapons of this time were swords, axes, and spears. Little armor beyond helm and shield was in evidence. Metal was still quite expensive at this time and only the wealthiest could afford additional armor. Bows were used upon occasion, but were not very powerful. Military formations were also rather rudimentary. A type of *shieldwall* was probably in use by this time. Warriors would lock together shields and form a long line. Two shieldwalls would meet and the first one to break would lose.

On the Continent, the Franks developed into the most vigorous of the Germanic tribes. By the eighth century, most of what would later become modern France was theirs, and they continually invaded Germany, Italy, and Spain. In fact, it was lucky for Europe that these Franks were so strong. A great threat to Europe was about to explode with the rise of Islam.

This new religion, founded by the prophet Mohammed, quickly spread across Asia, Africa, and even into Europe. Germanic kingdoms in North Africa and Spain quickly fell to these Islamic invaders, called Moslems.

A Moslem group called the Moors established bases in Spain and then invaded Frankish territory for plunder. A Frankish army under the leadership of Charles Martel met this Moorish army and fought them at Tours. The Moorish army was composed primarily of light cavalry, while the Franks of this age fought as infantry. Martel formed his troops in a long, steady line and prepared to receive the Moorish charge. The Franks had a throwing axe, called the *francisca*, which they used with great effect. The Moorish army attacked this wall and suffered heavily. The battle lasted until nightfall and the Moors were soundly defeated. They fled back to Spain, leaving behind their plunder.

By the end of the eighth century, *feudalism* was beginning to provide viable military organizations. Two major events provided impetus to feudalism: the invasions of the Magyars and the raids of the Vikings. They introduced new weapons and tactics, and also proved that the military organizations in place were unable to respond successfully to the new types of attacks.

The Magyars were an Asian tribe, which—in the nomadic tradition—relied upon swift, mounted attacks. For years the Magyars swept through virtually defenseless Eastern Europe, quite unchecked by the local militias. The Magyars presented a serious threat, but they were not a truly conquering army that threatened to overtake Europe. Instead, they were raiding parties, interested in plunder and slaves. They did, however, demonstrate the inefficiencies of the existing European military forces to deal with their attacks. Ultimately, the European kingdoms developed tactics to deal with these raiders. Fortifications were built, and the European heavy cavalry became more adept at intercepting the raiders. The organizations which hunted down the Magyars developed feudal ties.

However, almost simultaneously, a much more dangerous threat to established kingdoms came from the North in the final years of the eighth century. These were the Vikings or Norsemen. Overpopulation in the Scandinavian lands, a warlike society, and a strong desire for adventure and plunder sparked several centuries of raids and invasions that plagued Ireland, Scotland, England, and France; even Spain, Italy, North Africa, and Russia were hunting grounds for these fierce warriors.

Their initial forays struck terror into the hearts of their victims. In England, the violent Norsemen mercilessly slaughtered monks and plundered the Holy Island of Lindisfarne. The Vikings must have been amazed to dis-

The Vikings were sailors on the water and formidable soldiers when they disembarked on land. (By Manning de V. Lee, from Historic Ships, *by Rupert Sargent Holland, 1926)*

cover such a place of fantastic wealth completely undefended. The Vikings soon found dozens of other churches, retreats, and monasteries that were accessible from the sea and totally helpless. Monks often selected islands or remote coastal locations for their monasteries in order to escape from the mundane affairs of society. Unfortunately, while these sites were remote from the everyday affairs of their countrymen, they could not have been more accessible to the resourceful Vikings, who were the master sailors of their age.

With their sleek ships, the Vikings held a distinct technological advantage over their enemies. Viking longships were fast, narrow, and with a shallow draft—that is, they did not sit deep below the water line. As a result the longships could navigate the open ocean, prowl inland seas, or snake up rivers right into the heart of the invaded country. The Vikings were also known to halt in one river, then transport their entire ship across country to another body of water and continue their plundering of the unsuspecting countryside. The versatility of the Vikings was what perhaps made them so feared. They were not just sailors and pirates. Unlike the Magyars, who depended upon mobility and lightning raids, the Vikings were not at all daunted by walled cities and fortifications.

The earliest Viking raids were acts of piracy, but toward the middle of the ninth century they began to settle in conquered territory. Much of Ireland fell to them, as did the Orkneys, the Hebrides, part of the Scottish mainland, and vast sections of England and France. The Vikings were not just simple peasant warriors. They were an amalgamation of different types of people with different types of skills. For example, no one was their equal in the art of navigation. Four centuries before Columbus, Vikings had sailed across to the New World and established colonies. Among the Vikings were extremely skilled craftsmen, such as *shipwrights* and *armorers*. The Viking ships were the wonder of the age, and the Viking weapons were crafted with the same skill and patience.

Viking swords were famous for their strength and serviceability. Viking axes—huge weapons that were wielded with two hands and could cut a man in half—were dreaded weapons. The Vikings demanded quality, since the life of the owner often depended upon their not bending or breaking in the heat of battle. The *smiths* who crafted the weapons would engrave their own names in the blade, along with magical runic inscriptions, the name of the owner, or the name of the blade. Viking weapons were often given names like Odin's Flame or the Ice of Battle. Other Viking weapons were also given poetic names out of the Viking writings called *sagas*. Shields were known as the Battle-shelterer, or Net of the Spears. The huge axes were referred to as Fiend of the Shield or Would's Wolf. Spears were invariably known as serpents—"serpents of blood," for example.

Most Vikings wore a simple leather *byrnie* (a stiff garment that covered the upper torso) as armor. Leather was all the protection most warriors could afford. After a few raids, the luckier Vikings could afford to wear a coat of mail, flexible armor made up of many small pieces of metal. The picture one gets of both Viking and other warriors of this age is of a haphazardly clothed and armored group. The *helmets* played an important role in the identification of the Viking troops. A war mark was often painted on the helmet. This was a type of badge which helped the leaders identify their troops, since no distinguishing uniforms were used at the time. Hollywood aside, the Vikings did not wear the great horned helmets that are generally associated with them. The headgear of the leaders probably resembled the helm discovered at Sutton Hoo, an early Saxon burial site in England. The helm found there protected the entire head and had a face guard. However, since few Viking helmets survive, it is difficult to know what the average Viking wore.

In all probability, the Vikings made excellent use of captured weapons and armor. A phrase in the Anglo-Saxon poem, "The Battle of Maldon," refers to a *sutherna gar* (southern spear); this is believed to be a reference to a spear captured on a raid in France.

The early Viking warriors were magnificent soldiers, the best of their time. Because of them, the governments of Europe were forced to develop more effective countermeasures against invaders. Eventually, the feudal *knights* were able to meet the Vikings and prevent their depredations, but the Vikings remained a threat until the 10th and 11th centuries.

The early Viking warriors were generally any type of able-bodied man who could swing a sword and fit in with a ship's crew. But the Vikings also established true professional troops, the first since the fall of the Roman Empire in the West. These men were known as *Jomsvikings* (soldiers who lived in the fortress of Jomsborg). Strict military discipline was maintained. Only men of tried and true valor could apply—and no women were allowed in the fortress. Indeed, the age-old Viking ties of kinship were severed and the commander was given all allegiance.

Scandinavian kings controlled these warriors, who

were paid in coin of other countries. This was "protection money" or blackmail, and was known as *Danegeld*, paid to Vikings in return for a promise not to raid the area for a specific period of time. Huge sums of money were paid to these audacious blackmailers, who got just what they wanted—plunder without fighting for it. Eventually, King Cnut (or Canute) used the Jomsvikings to conquer all of England. Later the King of France ceded all of what is now known as Normandy to the Normans. (The word *Norman* is a corruption of *Norsemen*.)

By the 11th century, Viking raids had all but died out. A major reason was that the European kingdoms were no longer as weak as they had once been. The rise of feudalism had effectively cut off the Vikings' richest raiding grounds. Also, Vikings who had conquered territory and set up homesteads were none too eager to have their countrymen invade their new homelands. The Vikings who had settled in England and France often fought the stragglers who were bold enough to invade their territory.

During these invasions, European kingdoms began to develop a more effective means of dealing with incursions. In many countries there evolved a type of class system, with a hierarchy of power, along with a complex series of interrelationships that went beyond family, kingdom, and country. In essence, feudalism was based on the principle that a ruler of a country or domain granted sections of land (fiefdoms) in return for military service. The *vassals* (holders of fiefdoms) promised total loyalty to their *liege lord*. In reality, it was rarely that simple, and was more of an intricate patchwork quilt of relationships. For example, a noble was often both a vassal and liege lord at the same time—with the accompanying confusion in what action to take.

This type of situation eventually enabled the English king, Edward I, to claim title over Scotland. The Scottish kings and other Scottish nobles held large tracts of land in England. As English landowners, they owed allegiance to the English king, who granted the fiefdoms. Edward took that allegiance a step further, claiming that, since they owed homage for English lands, they owed homage in all areas—so Scotland was seen as a vassal country. Of course, the Scots did not view the situation that way and fought many bloody wars to prove that Scotland was not a northern province of England.

The feudal system had some intricate twists and turns, but it did succeed in creating a supply of very experienced soldiers who had a stake in fighting for the system in a particular area. The cream of the feudal fighting men in the medieval period were the armored, mounted *knights*, the supreme masters of heavy cavalry. Trained from childhood, these warriors were taught how to use the heavy *broadsword, lance, mace*, and axe from the back of a horse. Knighthood was an expensive proposition. Only the richest and most noble families could afford the costs incurred by knighthood. Armor, a trained charger, heavy weapons, and a troop of men-at-arms were all expensive. One German noble traded all of his land for a horse and sword.

One of the major battles between the old-style Germanic infantry and the newer armored cavalry occurred at the Battle of Hastings in 1066. The Normans, who had shed their Viking past and become the preeminent European cavalrymen, crossed the English Channel to meet the Anglo-Saxons. The Normans fought under the standard of William of Normandy, later known as the Conqueror. The English fought under the claimant to the throne of England, Harold of Wessex. England, isolated from the mainstream of European social evolution, had a mixed Anglo-Saxon, Scandinavian culture. Feudalism had not yet taken hold there. In warfare, the Anglo-Saxons relied upon the old traditions of fighting on foot behind the shieldwall. There were three distinct sections: the *housecarles*, a band of professional soldiers, who were the private guard of the king; the *fyrd*, a larger group made up of warriors called *thegns*, who were somewhat less well armored or trained than the housecarles; and the *great fyrd*, a mass of ill-armed peasantry who just added weight to the force.

The Norman force, on the other hand, was centered around the cavalry. The horsemen wore full-length mail garments and a steel helm with a nose guard. They carried a long slender lance, which was used for both stabbing and throwing, but their primary weapon was the broadsword. The Normans also had archers and infantry, many from Brittany. In a sense, the soldiers from Brittany were completing a circle. Centuries before, their ancestors had been forced to flee England by the invading Anglo-Saxons. They had left southern England and established new homes in France. The Anglo-Saxon kingdom that usurped their land was Wessex, and their soldiers returned to wrest a crown from a Wessex king.

The outcome of the Battle of Hastings was not a foregone conclusion, for the superiority of cavalry over infantry was far from proven. The English were fighting under tremendous disadvantages, however. Much of the English army had just marched south after crushing another invasion by the Norwegian king Harold Hardradda at the Battle of Stamford Bridge on September 26. The Battle of Hastings took place on October 14.

Harold, with his uneven infantry, drew up his force in a shieldwall, housecarles in the center and fyrd members on the wings. The Normans, who slightly outnumbered

Crossing the English Channel, these Norman soldiers took their indispensable horses. (From the Bayeux Tapestry, authors' archives)

the English, attacked in three separate lines. The first line was composed of archers, the second line the infantry, and the third line the Norman cavalry. The archers advanced up the hill, followed by the infantry. The bows they used were short and generally ineffective. Since they did little damage to the English infantry, the archers fell back and allowed the infantry to come to hand grips with the English. The Norman infantry was no match for the English in their defensive positions. Wielding huge, two-handed axes, swords, and spears, the English infantry pushed back the Norman infantry. Then the Norman cavalry charged—and had the same lack of success as the infantry.

Then a turning point in the battle occurred. The Norman cavalry turned and fled. Some historians have considered this a feigned flight; others have said it was real. It makes little difference, since the ultimate effect was the same and gave William a victory. As the horsemen fled, many of the fyrdsmen broke ranks and pursued them, thinking victory won. But the Normans, having lured the English out of their lines, turned and cut them to pieces. The battle was fought for several more hours, with Harold's housecarles standing like rocks against the combined assaults of Norman cavalry, infantry, and archers. But by nightfall, Harold had been killed and the English army destroyed. William had conquered England and brought the kingdom into the feudal fold. The Normans who accompanied him were granted tracts of land throughout England, forming the new ruling class in the land.

The Normans were highly successful conquerors. During the 11th and 12th centuries, they added to Normandy and England much of France, parts of Italy, and Ireland. A far-reaching event, which affected European military evolution, occurred at the height of their power. The tolerant Fatimid rulers of Jerusalem were overthrown by fanatic Seljuks, who began to persecute Christian pilgrims to the Holy Land. Pope Urban II called for a holy war to free the lands from the infidel Moslems—and so the *Crusades* were born.

The Crusaders

For the most part, the Crusades were a series of ill-conceived, bungled affairs, which hardly presented a unified front of Christian might to the Moslems in the Middle East. The only truly successful military crusades were the First and Third Crusades. In most, a loose confederation of European nobles gathered their armies and proceeded to try to liberate the Holy Land.

The First Crusade was, to a large extent, a Norman affair. With some dubious aid from the Byzantine Empire, Western European armies invaded the Holy Land. They had little idea of what they were getting themselves into. By all rights the crusade should have been a dismal failure. Almost every step of the way was blocked by some new hardship. The Europeans were used to foraging for supplies and had no real supply system. The troops were often on the verge of starvation. They also had little experience fighting the swift Asiatic horsemen, who quickly fired arrows and then disappeared. However, the Europeans had one advantage: their heavily armored horsemen. Initially the Moslems tried to meet them openly, and were generally ridden down for their pains. The heavily armored Europeans were often victorious against much larger Moslem forces. Against all odds, the Europeans carved out several kingdoms in the Middle East, even taking the city of Jerusalem.

The European knight was, individually, the supreme warrior of the age. Heavily armored—the helmet alone could weigh between 15 and 20 pounds—and wielding heavy weapons, such as sword and mace, no other type of warrior could stand singly against him. The Moslems had magnificent weapons themselves. Their *scimitars*, beautifully balanced with fine Damascus steel, were far superior in quality to Western blades. Yet these light weapons could not slice through the Europeans' armor, while the Crusaders' heavy weapons could smash through the Moslems' fine but light armor.

Eventually, the Crusaders were evicted from the Middle East. More powerful, more numerous Moslem armies learned how to take advantage of Western weaknesses. The Saracen leader Saladin, for example, used a tactic which separated Western knights from their infantry; this allowed his more numerous horsemen to defeat each arm in turn. The individual fighting soldier, no matter how good, could not stand against far superior Moslem tactics and strength.

There was a total of about eight different crusades, depending upon how they are counted. The fall of the city of Acre in 1291 removed the last European holding in the Middle East. Little more than 200 years had passed since the start of the First Crusade. During that time, the Western kingdoms learned much about Moslem and Byzantine culture and science, both of which were far in advance of the Europeans'. In the military arts, the returning Crusaders copied and even improved upon the advanced fortification of the Byzantines. They also rediscovered the necessity of supply. Kings, such as Richard I of England, established bases and began to pay more attention to keeping their troops well fed. New tactics were also developed. The single-minded approach to war, in which armed groups just rode at each other and the strongest won, was slowly replaced by more intricate plans of attack. Byzantine and Moslem approaches to war, with feints and stratagems, were adapted to Western use.

As a result, although the Crusades were ultimately a major failure, the Europeans learned some very important lessons. The Crusades also provided a backdrop to a continuing Moslem-Christian struggle for supremacy. Many Moslem conquerors would attempt to sweep into Europe over the next several centuries. The most successful would be the Ottoman Turks, who took Constantinople and captured much of Eastern Europe.

The armies of the Middle Ages used much the same type of weapons as had the ancients, albeit usually less sophisticated and less efficient. There were notable exceptions, however. The Europeans used the crossbow very effectively and also a new, very powerful weapon, the *trebuchet*, based on a unique method of propulsion employing gravity. Possibly invented in China, it made its way to Europe by the early part of the Middle Ages. This remarkable war machine contained a basket of weights—rocks, metal, any heavy junk—fastened to a long arm or shaft. When the trigger was released, the weights would suddenly drop, whipping the connected arm up. With an attached sling to add to the whip, the projectile could be fired with tremendous velocity.

These trebuchet could fling a much larger projectile than any other engine of war. In fact, this simple weapon was limited only by the size of the arm and the amount of weight that could be gathered together. It is well documented that some trebuchets could hurl a 300-pound boulder over 300 yards. There are also references to dead horses and luckless human beings launched into towns by these weapons. The trebuchet was an effective weapon that was very simple to make—wood and rocks and rope were almost all that was needed. This machine coexisted with the cannon for centuries, while firearms were gaining dominance, and even made a few appearances after cannons had become fully accepted. At the siege of Rhodes in 1480, trebuchet opposed Turkish cannon and caused heavy casualties. As late as 1780, the English joy-rigged a trebuchet to repulse a combined French and Spanish attack upon Gibraltar. The innovative English troops devised a trebuchet that could cast a stone at a high angle, to dislodge the enemy hidden among the rocks.

Eastern Armies

The beginning of the 13th century witnessed the rise of one of the most awesome military organizations ever created: the Mongols. The Mongol people had been another in a long series of herders occupying the barren lands north of China's magnificent Great Wall. Like their predecessors, they were for most of their history organized in a series of constantly warring tribes. However, in the late 12th century, Temujin, later known as Genghis Khan, unified the Mongol tribes, welding them into a single kingdom. After that, Genghis Khan turned to China and proceeded to conquer it. By 1215, the Mongols had made their way past the Great Wall and had sacked Peking. The Chin emperor recognized the Mongols as his overlords. Over the next 13 years, the Mongols under Genghis Khan and his officers conquered most of Asia. They smashed the Chinese kingdoms and advanced into Russia. By the time Genghis Khan died in 1227, the Mongols had established a huge Eurasian empire.

In the 13th century Russians (on the left) and Mongols battled for control of the region around Kiev. (New York Public Library)

The conquests continued under the khan's successors, who invaded Europe, the Middle East, and even Japan. Russia and Eastern Europe particularly suffered at the hands of the Mongols. They laid waste to all of north-central Europe from the Baltic Sea to the Carpathian Mountains. They virtually destroyed Hungary, Bulgaria, and Serbia. They did, at last, withdraw from Europe, but for several centuries they stayed in Russia, which was under the administration of the Golden Horde.

Japan was much luckier. The Japanese, like the Europeans of the time, had developed a type of feudal structure. They also glorified the individual warrior, who fought for honor in one-to-one combat. The Mongols on two occasions invaded Japan. The first invasion was a reconnaissance, in which the outnumbered Mongols made short work of a Japanese army. However, they were soon forced to return to the mainland. Kublai Khan later ordered a full-scale invasion of Japan. The Japanese outnumbered the Mongols, but the Mongols still were winning when a storm destroyed the Mongol fleet. Cut off, the Mongol army was destroyed and Japan was saved from almost certain conquest.

As a result of the Mongol failure, the Japanese were left to develop their own militaristic culture. It was a rigid class structure, which worshipped the armed might of individual soldiers, the *samurai*. These warriors allied themselves with various clans and engaged in warfare with other clans.

The Japanese weapons were of the highest quality, with very effective single-edged blades. Primarily *swordsmen*, the samurai developed a ritualistic and rigid code to go with their fine weapons. When Japan was finally unified in the 17th century, after centuries of civil war, the samurai turned their sights toward Korea, which they viewed as a step toward taking China. However, the Koreans, with support of the Chinese, limited Japanese successes. And the Korean navy proved to be far more effective than the Japanese fleet. In the end the Japanese had to withdraw.

During this time, Europeans were also just testing their strength in Japan. They gained a few footholds, but ultimately, the Japanese expelled the Europeans, afraid of contamination from Western weapons and culture. It was not until 1854, when the American fleet opened up Japan to the West, that Japan left its feudal period behind.

The early Mongol army was almost exclusively composed of hardy horsemen, who were extremely well trained and well organized. The descriptive term *horde* is not quite accurate. The Mongols were not just bodies of fierce cavalry that appeared like a plague and then disappeared. They often were outnumbered by their enemies. However, the speed with which they struck and their swirling tactics often led the enemy to believe that they had far more soldiers than they really had.

The cavalry was divided into light and heavy units. The heavy cavalry was armored and used for shock action. Their primary weapon was the lance. The light cavalry made up most of the force. They were lightly armored and carried a powerful reflex bow with two quivers of arrows. In some assaults, the heavy cavalry would dismount and attack as infantry. All troopers carried a sword or axe, in addition to the lance or bow. These steppe tribesmen were very hardy people. They could ride great distances without rest. They also had little need of complex supply trains. As a last resort, the Mongol riders would open a vein in their horse and drink the blood for nourishment. The basic unit of the horde was the *touman*, a group of 10,000 soldiers. Three toumans made up an army division. Each touman had ten regiments of 1,000 warriors each. The smallest body was a squadron with ten warriors.

After conquering China, Genghis Khan was able to draw on that civilized country's reservoir of technologists and engineers. Originally stymied by fortifications, Genghis Khan copied Chinese methods and provided the Mongol armies with an added dimension. A train of Chinese engineers accompanied the hordes and provided the genius for capturing fortified cities. In this regard, they were far more dangerous than the Magyars and Huns, who had had no siege talent.

The Mongols used terror as a tactic—and may even have outdone the bloody Assyrians in their barbarity. Cities that resisted were often put to the sword, with hundreds of thousands slaughtered. However, the Mongols were quite lenient to those who capitulated and would work with them. The Mongol Empire lasted for several hundred years in parts of Asia, because they developed an efficient administration along Chinese lines.

The Mongols used all types of tactics and stratagems in fighting their enemies. They were extremely adept at discovering weaknesses in their opponents. They were also masters of the feint, of finding ways to deceive their opponents and catch them off guard. At the Battle of the Sajó River, a body of Mongols held off a large Hungarian army, while the main body outflanked the Hungarians, attacking them in the side and rear and killing up to 70,000 of them.

In the end, the Mongols left little lasting impression upon the societies they conquered. Magnificent in warfare, agile in battle and conquest, they had little of value to offer the occupied countries and were finally absorbed by the native peoples.

Later European Armies

The beginning of the end of the feudal knight came in the 14th century. In 1302, proud French knights were slaughtered as they became entangled in a swampy area fighting despised Flemish burghers at the Battle of Courtrai. This was ignored as a fluke, but it was a major defeat of a strong cavalry army overpowered by infantry. Then in 1314, a Scottish army, composed mainly of rugged spearmen, destroyed an English army, which contained the best of English knighthood, at the Battle of Bannockburn. In this battle, the tactical skill of the Scottish king, Robert the Bruce, took advantage of

Displaying their heraldry, these knights are participating in a jousting tournament. (From Diderot's Encyclopedia, *late 18th century)*

English King Edward II's mistake in deploying his forces. The Scottish spearmen in tight formation, known as *schiltrons*, advanced down toward the tightly packed English. The ground was too marshy to allow effective cavalry charges, so the knights dismounted. They were broken by the tough Scottish spearmen and ultimately routed.

The shock waves began to form. The English themselves introduced a devastating weapon which hurried the demise of the armored cavalry. This was the *longbow*, thought to have been developed in Wales. The English king Edward I quickly recognized its importance and incorporated it into his armies. The use of this weapon was refined in the long and bloody Scottish wars of independence. The English would use the bow to tear gaps in the lines of Scottish spearmen in preparation for a cavalry charge.

The longbow was a particularly difficult weapon to master, being nearly six feet long, in many cases, and with a draw weight of up to—or even beyond—100 pounds. It took a very powerful man to fire this weapon—and training from boyhood to master it. This is why only England was able to maintain large numbers of longbow archers in the field. The *yeomanry* (small landowners) of England grew up with the bow and supplied a steady reservoir of talent to swell the ranks of English archers.

The bow itself was very effective. It could fire a cloth yard shaft over 400 yards and still pierce light armor. At shorter ranges it would punch right through mail and some plate. The cloth yard shaft was the type of arrow used, generally three feet long; the old rule was that the bow should be as long as the user was tall and that the arrow should be half as long as the bow.

The longbow was suddenly introduced into France at the start of the Hundred Years War. It made its debut at the Battle of Crécy in 1346. In this battle, the English force of about 20,000 defeated a French force of two to three times its size. The French force had the best of the land's nobility in the van—the foremost position in the army—more than 13,000 knights and men-at-arms. The French force also had several thousand Genoese mercenary *crossbowmen*—the crossbow being a stiff, short bow, mounted on a stock and shot by squeezing a trigger—and a large number of ragtag, levied infantry.

The French were supremely confident that they would be able to crush the upstart English army. Philip VI, king of France, began the battle by sending his crossbowmen

Machines like this one could hurl missiles of great weight and destructive power. (From Diderot's Encyclopedia, *late 18th century*)

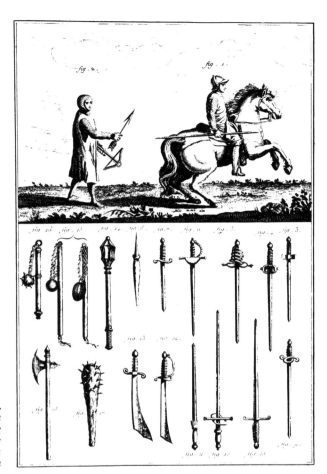

Before the development of firearms, soldiers had available to them a wide range of weapons, including those at the bottom and the crossbow at top left. (From Diderot's Encyclopedia, *late 18th*

forward against the English line. The English had three *battles* (divisions), one on the right, one on the left, and one to the rear. The English men-at-arms had dismounted and stood beside the archers. The rear battle was mounted and under the direct command of King Edward III ready to counterattack any French successes.

The French had no success. First, their Genoese crossbowmen were a dismal failure. A squall had wet their weapons' strings and reduced their effective range. Even without rain, the result probably would have been the same. The longbow's rate of fire and range were much greater than the crossbow's. As the Genoese marched into range, the English archers mowed them down with thick flights of arrows.

The impatient French knights then made the serious error of charging into the retreating rabble of crossbowmen. This threw their lines into confusion and made them easy targets for the English archers. The heavy English shafts tore through their mail protection, killing dozens of men and horses. This body of knights retreated and then another body of French cavalry insanely charged the virtually untouched English lines, which poured volley after volley into the stubborn French. The battle lasted until nightfall, when the French quit the field. They lost nearly 20,000 men. The English lost about 200. The knight of chivalry was rapidly becoming an endangered species.

The next invention to speed the demise of the armored knight was the *firearm*. This weapon gave the lowliest soldier the means to kill the highest and mightiest lord in his full armor. Firearms affected the development of a variety of occupations. The use of the new weapon and defenses against it were experimented with. The heavily armored cavalry evolved into new types of horsemen that were less protected and depended upon speed together with the new firearm.

The invention of the *wheelock*—in which a small wheel was turned against flint to produce sparks, and so ignite gunpowder—allowed the creation of a firearm that could be held with one hand and fired with effect from horseback. The Germans introduced cavalrymen who were armed with a new weapon known as a *pistol*. They would ride at the enemy in thick columns. When they were within range, they would empty their pistols at the enemy, then the front ranks would wheel around and gallop to the rear, where they would reload and wait for another turn while the other ranks performed the same maneuver. This was called the *caracole*. In theory, it was a fine tactic. However, its success was limited. As long as the enemy stayed in place, the caracole could work. A strong counterattack would throw off the delicate timing and break the formation.

Guns became useful weapons for the cavalry. For the next several centuries, however, an argument waged over whether to use guns or rely upon the traditional lance and sword. For the most part, the old shock tactics were maintained, but the gun had made a mark and remained as an adjunct weapon in many units.

The history of fortification and siegecraft was also rewritten with the introduction of gunpowder. Gunpowder made possible a new type of *artillery*, mounted guns with which the French were able to capture a series of English-held castles in a matter of months—castles that would have taken years to capture using the old methods. And the colossal event of the 15th century was the relatively quick collapse of Constantinople to the Ottoman Turks, after it had survived many prolonged sieges over more than a thousand years. Although thinly defended, the great city could never have been taken had the Turks not used a great train of the most advanced artillery of the time to tear holes in the city's venerable walls. *Cannon* were introduced to fire heavier, more destructive types of projectiles. Smaller cannon were also used on the battlefield.

In the 14th century, Jan Žižka's peasant Czech followers—the Hussites—mounted guns on wagons. The Hussites drew their wagons into a defensive *laager* (circle) when attacked. It was one of the first uses of cannon as a mobile arm, in conjunction with the rest of the army. Later, cannons were mounted on carriages and drawn by horses or oxen into the battlefield. In 1515, the Battle of Marignano, which pitted French artillery against the then-dominant Swiss infantry, proved to be a major military turning point. The Swiss attacked in their traditional lines of *pikemen*, with their usual daring and skill. But the French artillery was able to cut huge gaps in the Swiss lines. The gallant Swiss fought on for two days, but in the end they were forced to sue for peace—after losing thousands of men to the efficient French guns.

Ist das der danck/vnd vnser Soldt/
   So sey der teüfel dem Kryeg holdt/
Erfars ein ander/ich biñ satt/
   Mir hat man zogen schoh/roch/matt.

This soldier is being held still while the surgeon attempts to extract an arrowhead from his chest—without benefit of any anesthetic. (By Johannes Wechtlin, from Feldtbuch der Wundartzney, 1540*)*

The operators of the artillery—the *gunners*—were highly respected soldiers during the time of the Battle of Marignano. Firing artillery took a prodigious amount of skill. The art of determining range and properly elevating the barrel took substantial grounding in mathematics. Cities and commanders would hire gunners, who often worked as mercenaries, to help create new weapons and defenses. In fact, no European army could afford to be without these specialists when they engaged in both open battles and siege warfare.

Renaissance scientists eagerly involved themselves with the theories behind artillery. Leonardo da Vinci performed some experiments in determining *trajectory*, the path of a projectile. Later, in the early part of the 16th century, a famous Italian mathematician, Niccolo Tartaglia, also studied the movement of projectiles. Tartaglia proved that once a projectile is fired from the barrel, it immediately begins to fall. From this significant discovery, the whole science of *ballistics* evolved.

As artillery developed, the opposing principle could not afford to stagnate. The science of fortification steadily improved. Castles, which had been dominant for centuries, were relegated to a colorful past. The problem of the day was to defend against the wall-shattering power of artillery. Again, the best and brightest of their age developed fortifications. Da Vinci, Tartaglia, Machiavelli, and many others theorized about the best defenses against sieges.

One reason the giants of science engaged in developing this type of warfare was that it was new and exciting. Although there was little difference in the ultimate design of a pre-gunpowder and post-gunpowder siege, the new gunpowder had such devastating power that the whole concept of defense had to be reexamined.

The writing was on the wall when Charles VIII of France marched through Italy in the late 15th century, quickly destroying strong castles with his train of artillery. Fortifications could no longer offer such easy targets. The high medieval walls were lowered and thickened. Many different types of building materials were experimented with. The fortress was created to make the fullest use of natural surroundings, such as lakes, streams, and hills. Earthworks were thrown up to cushion the shock of opposing gunfire. Different types of geometric patterns were used in the design of the new forts. The architects invented fortifications that would be protected not only against opposing artillery fire, but also against direct assault of enemy infantry. To accomplish this mission, the designers determined the best fields of fire and built strongly emplaced *batteries* from which gunners could defend the fort from infantry charges.

The new fortresses were very strong and were seemingly as invulnerable to existing gunpowder artillery as the old castles had been to the ancient siege weapons. This did not last for long, but one example of how a new fort held up under a powerful siege was seen in Rhodes in 1522. The city of Rhodes, defended by the Knights Hospitallers of St. John's, had been redesigned in the new fashion of fortification. Led by Grand Master Philip Villiers de L'Isle Adam were 700 knights and 6,000 light troops. The Turks, led by Sultan Suleiman I, eventually used over 200,000 men during the siege, which began in June of 1522 and lasted until the end of the year. The Turks, using artillery and frontal assaults, lost between 50,000 and 100,000 men trying to take this magnificent fort. However, the Turkish barrage was also telling. By December, the Turks were able to force their way into the city, only to be contained and repulsed by the greatly weakened Hospitallers.

The fortress was never taken by feats of arms. Suleiman, horrified by the cost in his soldiers' lives, negotiated an honorable surrender. At the end, 180 knights and 1,500 other troops filed out of the city with their weapons and left Rhodes in the hands of the Turks. Few armies were as willing as those of the Turks to squander lives. Rhodes would probably not have been taken if any of the powerful European kingdoms had reinforced the Hospitallers. Instead, against the overwhelming might of the Ottoman Empire, it fell.

The height of European fortification and siege warfare

In this view of life in the Middle Ages, the military plays an important part, massed as cavalry and laying siege to a fort. (Woodcut after Sebastian Brant, from Publii Virgilii Maronis Opera, *1502)*

was reached in the 17th century during the reign of Louis XIV. His master engineer, Sébastien de Vauban, created systems for building and besieging fortifications that were ardently studied until the 19th century. Vauban went beyond the static concept of forts as defensive structures. He constructed a series of fortifications throughout France that also served as mighty depots for the army as it prepared to advance into other countries.

Vauban did not introduce any radically new methods, but he was known as a master of obtaining the most from the natural surroundings. He was a master of detail, and used his mathematical skill in creating highly effective battery placements.

Vauban was also the master of the siege. Under the tutelage of Vauban and some of his contemporaries, the armies of Europe learned how to assault successfully the strong new fortifications. For example, Vauban invented a method of attacking in parallel against a specific spot in the besieged fort, generally the weakest spot in its construction. These weak spots were often scouted out by Vauban himself before the arrival of the French army. Trenches would be dug and, under cover, the besiegers would advance closer and closer. Artillery was brought up by the attackers and eventually was positioned very near to the weakest point of the fort. It soon became apparent to the defenders that the attacking force could breach the wall. Often, at this stage, the defenders would surrender without any further fighting. In fact, during the 17th and 18th centuries, siegecraft became almost a

Early modern warfare involved massive numbers of soldiers and armaments against huge engineered fortresses; note burning towns in background. (Attributed to Albrecht Dürer, early 16th century)

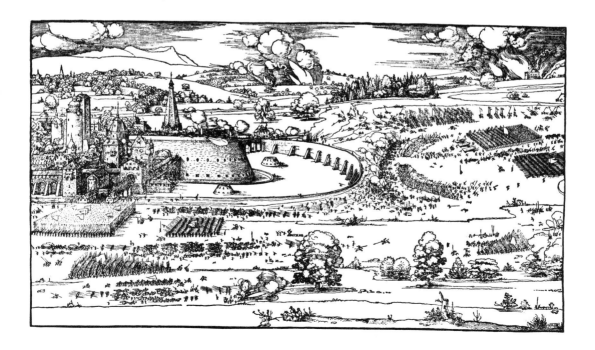

ritualized game. The commander would often surrender without any last-ditch stands and often well before any major assaults were launched, once a predetermined section of ground was taken by the besieging force.

Many different types of occupations developed along with new fortifications. At the highest level, the engineering geniuses, such as Vauban, could even change the military policy of a country's armed forces. There were also *architects, artisans, contractors*, and *laborers* who built the structures. Within the more strictly military occupations, specialized forms of troops manned the fortifications. These garrisons were the dregs of the military in some armies. The old and infirm or even criminally inclined would be given the responsibility for occupying the fort. Only during times of war would these lowly garrisons be reinforced by regular troops. However, some armies recognized the importance of having a well-trained force garrisoning the forts at all times. The French troops under Vauban held a more responsible position, possibly because he viewed the French fortifications as important elements in a more unified military organization. Indeed, Vauban was quite concerned that the fortress garrisons be kept happy and in good shape. In addition to keeping his troops well fed, Vauban made sure that they were also able to get plenty of tobacco.

In Europe, the 17th century was an age of transition in terms of military evolution. The last vestiges of the Middle Ages died during this period. Pikemen and archers were almost universally replaced by *musketeers*. (*Muskets* were heavy smooth-bored shoulder guns that shot a single ball.) The heavily armored knight was gone from the field of battle and only made an occasional appearance in tournaments. Technology at last gained the upper hand. Technical artisans continued to play a major part in improving existing weapons and coming up with better designs. The casting process for artillery pieces became much more refined. New locks and mechanisms for muskets were invented, enabling the musket, and later the rifle, to become much more deadly in the hands of a trained marksman.

However, the major upheaval at this time was not in individual military occupations, but rather in the development of military organizations on a large scale. The 17th century witnessed the first appearance of truly modern armies. At this time, monarchs began demanding large standing armies, expensive though they were. These armies, with their new weapons, became increasingly destructive, and the 17th century saw some devastating wars.

This was the time of the Thirty Years' War, a terrible conflict fought roughly between 1618 and 1648. During this time, huge standing armies were created, and battles became larger. Even more modern, civilians suffered greatly. Some historians estimate that during this period the various duchies and kingdoms of what is now modern Germany lost up to a third of their population to warfare, starvation, and disease.

At the beginning of the 17th century, armies rarely exceeded 40,000 or 50,000 troops. By the end of the century, armies of more than 100,000 were common. Troops, by the end of the century, tended to be members of a royal army loyal to their regent—a step toward the modern army, with loyalty toward the homeland. This meant that these soldiers had to be treated differently from troops levied for short periods of time. Soldiers remained soldiers the year round; they were finally full-time employees of the state.

The introduction of the large standing army also meant that a great deal more money had to be raised to support it. New *barracks* had to be constructed and organizations had to be made more uniform. Weapons became standardized, so soldiers could be sure that their compatriots used the identical weapons and ammunition. *Ranks* were standardized, and cohesive, efficient forces were developed. The modern army was in the process of being born, rivaling the organizations of ancient Rome.

One special development, which illustrates how the

armed forces were being welded into a more standardized organization with purpose and loyalty, was the creation of the *uniform*. Before the 17th century, soldiers could identify their own troops in a variety of ways. Sometimes warriors in the same force wore badges or tokens for identification. Scottish Highlanders of the same clan wore a plant badge in their bonnets. During the Middle Ages, different households and even kingdoms adopted standards and symbols for identification. The art of *heraldry* grew out of this. However, even the Romans, though they wore the same

In the East, cannons were sometimes slung on the backs of camels, as here. (From Diderot's Encyclopedia, *late 18th century)*

armor and had standardized weapons, did not have what can be considered true uniforms.

During the beginning of the Thirty Years' War, there was almost a chaotic appearance in the armies, when various groups of mercenaries continued to wear their own colors. Then Gustavus Adolphus, king of Sweden, introduced uniform colors for his own soldiers—a distinctive color for each regiment: blue, yellow, and green. In England, Oliver Cromwell introduced the traditional scarlet of the British uniform in the middle of the 17th century. And by the end of the century, most European countries had adopted some type of uniform for their various regiments.

With the introduction of the uniform, the appearance of Europe's soldiers was hardly dull in comparison to warriors of earlier ages. On the contrary, bright, easily identified colors were the rule rather than the exception. The handsome, well-turned regiments were the pride of their rulers. The soldiers learned to march into deadly hails of bullets and cannon in parade-ground fashion. It must have been a colorful sight. However, the invention of the rifle and more accurate weapons would later, in the 19th century, prove to be too much for the colorful uniforms. Armies could no longer afford to present such gaudy targets to sharpshooters firing at specific targets from long distances.

The 17th century saw both the flowering and fall of mercenary forces. During the Thirty Years' War, armies of several thousand mercenaries roamed Europe. Hired soldiers, who have had a great impact upon the organization of countless numbers of armies, had existed throughout history. Probably from the earliest times, there were skilled warriors who were eager to sell their skills to rulers who were just as eager to buy. Often mercenaries offered a particular skill for sale. For example, Greek armies hired slingers and archers to add another dimension to the hoplite-dominated forces. Roman armies also made use of Balearic slingers, Aegean archers, and North African cavalry. They also hired barbarians in the later stages of the empire—and all through the existence of the empire many Romans obtained fierce Germans as bodyguards. Even the Moors of North Africa used Christian knights called *Frendji* (for Franks) as their private guards.

Indeed, mercenaries were important not only because of their skills but also because they had no political axes to grind. Paid well, they supported the most unpopular monarchs and protected them from the wrath of the populace. The Swiss were well known as hirelings willing to fight for almost anyone, if the price was right. At times, they ran out of luck, when political events overtook them. During the French Revolution, the Swiss were marked as symbols of the old regime and subject to mob killings. Unfortunately, mercenaries could also become two-edged swords that cut their employers. King Vortigern of post-Roman Britain hired German mercenaries to fight the Picts and Scots. But the Germans then turned on Vortigern and conquered much of Britain. The Swiss also were fickle at times. In some campaigns, they were bribed

The Bloody Massacre perpetrated in King — Street Boston on March 5 1770 by a party of the 29 Reg.t

Unhappy Boston! see thy Sons deplore,
Thy hallow'd Walks besmear'd with guiltless Gore.
While faithless P—n and his savage Bands,
With murd'rous Rancour stretch their bloody Hands;
Like fierce Barbarians grinning o'er their Prey,
Approve the Carnage, and enjoy the Day.

If scalding drops from Rage from Anguish Wrung
If speechless Sorrows lab'ring for a Tongue,
Or if a weeping World can ought appease
The plaintive Ghosts of Victims such as these;
The Patriot's copious Tears for each are shed,
A glorious Tribute which embalms the Dead.

But know, Fate summons to that awful Goal,
Where Justice strips the Murd'rer of his Soul;
Should venal C—ts the scandal of the Land,
Snatch the relentless Villain from her Hand,
Keen Execrations on this Plate inscrib'd,
Shall reach a Judge who never can be brib'd.

Engrav'd Printed & Sold by Paul Revere Boston

The unhappy Sufferers were Mess.rs Sam.l Gray, Sam.l Maverick, Jam.s Caldwell, Crispus Attucks & Pat.k Carr
Killed. Six wounded; two of them (Christ.r Monk & John Clark) Mortally

not to fight; this generally had a very detrimental effect on the fighting ability of their employer's army.

On the other hand, mercenaries at times provided a level of skill which native troops could not supply. For example, the Norman invasion of Ireland was pathetically

In the Boston Massacre, British "redcoats" shot and killed five Colonials, four whites and one black. (By Paul Revere, from the Boston Gazette, March 12, 1770)

Firearms gave soldiers an immediate advantage, which this Portuguese man turned toward slave hunting. (British Museum, Benin bronze sculpture, c. 1600)

easy in the initial going because the lightly armored Irish were no match for the heavily armored Normans and their Welsh auxiliaries. The Normans met and easily destroyed several Irish armies. Ultimately, the Irish chieftains hired Scottish mercenaries from the Hebrides. Known as *galloglasses*, these warriors were as fierce and as heavily armored as the Normans. With a unique mixture of Celtic and Scandinavian fighting talents, they held the Normans to a standstill. For centuries to come, Irish chieftains used these troops to fight the Normans, the English, and, of course, one another.

During times of social upheaval, mercenaries were

numerous. In the Thirty Years' War, a substantial portion of the armies were mercenaries. The Swedish army, which had many native Swedes, also contained substantial contingents of Scottish mercenaries, from lowly foot soldiers to the highest commanders. The German leader Wallenstein contracted an entire mercenary army to the Catholic States of Europe. The French had their Scots, Irish, and Swiss troops. Traditionally, mercenaries come from poor countries with a surplus of healthy manpower. Countries such as Switzerland, Germany, Scotland, Ireland, and Wales have been major suppliers of mercenaries to armies around the world. John Paul Jones, born a poor Scot, was a hero in the American Revolution and served as an admiral in the Russian navy.

Armies in the Americas

In the same period, the colonization of new lands around the world brought Europeans into often violent conflict with other cultures and military establishments. For example, the French, British, and Spanish in the Americas came into contact with the Native Americans. The Spanish quickly destroyed the native Central and South American armies that protected highly developed civilizations. The Aztecs and Incas could field large, well-organized armies in the 16th century, but they lacked the weapons to halt the Spanish.

In North America, the Native Americans fought in more limited, *guerrilla* style. For the most part, the tribes the Europeans faced—the Iroquois, Hurons, and Creeks—fought as irregulars. Brave, able to move swiftly through thick forests on foot, and skilled in woodlore, they proved to be elusive foes. However, they were doomed to failure in their many struggles with the Europeans because of lack of numbers, inferior weapons, and the fact that they often were more interested in fighting each other than the colonists.

By the 18th century, the Europeans had learned to enlist various tribes to their own cause. The British, who were at odds with the French, enlisted the aid of the Iroquois, while the French joined forces with Hurons and other tribes. Many battles in the slinking, skirmishing style were fought in the New World. Although regular line formations were used, irregular skirmishes became common even between trained European military organizations in the New World.

The British and French adopted this style of fighting one another during the so-called French and Indian Wars, in which both sides often had substantial numbers of colonists and Native Americans in their ranks. At the Battle of Quebec on the Plains of Abraham in 1759, the English general James Wolfe was rewarded when his new light infantry found a path up to the battlefield which outflanked the French defenses. The British troops then slaughtered the attacking French forces with highly accurate musket and rifle fire. Both commanding officers died in this battle, but the British prevailed and went on to win Canada.

From the 16th through 19th centuries, European and later American forces clashed with the native warriors of the New World. They quickly destroyed the most organized cultures, but the fierceness of various tribes provided the colonists with a great deal of trouble. The tribes that fought against the encroaching settlers were from various cultures with different languages. The Europeans never really faced a foe united in resistance or culture. The Native Americans fought in various ways, too. Tribes such as the Comanches and Sioux were among the finest light cavalry troops in the world. Horses, introduced to the New World by the Spanish, were quickly adopted by many tribes—especially those who lived on the vast western plains. This gave them an astonishing degree of mobility. Other tribes, such as the Apaches and Seminoles, were master infantry guerrilla fighters. They could range long distances and strike viciously and swiftly. The Apache leader Geronimo was a highly

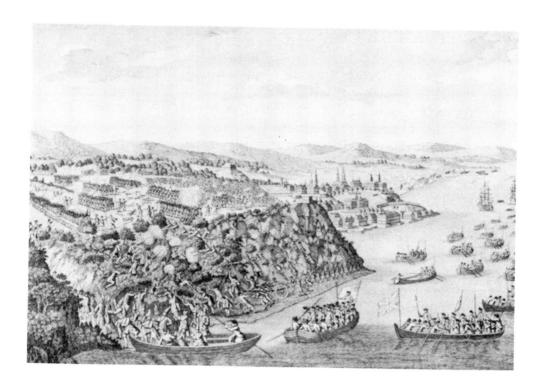

talented commander, striking terror through the American Southwest.

At the start of their struggles with the Europeans, Native Americans had only primitive weapons. Stone hatchets, weak bows, and lances were their primary arms. Some of the plains tribes developed leather armor. After the arrival of the Europeans, trade and capture provided tribes with more modern weapons, from steel *tomahawks* bartered by fur traders to firearms. The tomahawk, like the Frankish *francisca*, was an effective throwing and striking weapon.

In the end, the Native Americans were overpowered by a more technically advanced European culture that was none too scrupulous in how it obtained lands. As white civilization pushed westward, few treaties were honored, and the massacre of Native American villages under treaty grew commonplace.

The English defeated the French at Quebec by landing upstream behind the fortress city and fighting on the Plains of Abraham. (Public Archives of Canada, 1759)

The 19th Century

The enormous social and technical changes during the 19th century greatly affected military occupations. The late 18th and early 19th centuries were an age of revolutions. Some were political—the American, South American and French revolutions, for example. Another was technical; the Industrial Revolution of this period created enormous technological advances, which turned the world upside down and had a tremendous impact on military forces.

A comparison of the military forces of Europe and America at the beginning of the 19th century with their counterparts at the end of the century shows the enormous changes effected. For example, the infantry at the start of the century still, for the most part, relied upon smooth-bore, muzzle-loading muskets. These weapons had a short effective range and were slow-loading. To obtain the greatest effect, the infantry was taught to fire in lines in volleys. There was little aimed fire, because the soldiers were generally firing at other massed groups of infantry or cavalry. By the end of the century, many weapons were still single shot but most were breech-loading—that is, they were loaded at the rear of the barrel, like modern guns, rather than at the front, like earlier guns. Most armies had, however, adopted magazine rifles with bolt actions, in which several shots might be stored in a compartment called a *magazine* and then fed into the firing chamber. These enabled the soldier to fire several times without reloading. These weapons were also rifled—that is, spiral grooves cut in the bore caused the shot to spin; as a result these weapons had a much greater range, and were far more accurate than the muskets.

The 19th century also witnessed a host of inventions that changed the face of warfare and reshaped military occupations. New, more powerful explosives, the railroad, the steam engine, the telegraph, and rapid-fire guns, such as the *Gatling gun*—transformed warfare. The armies grew in size and efficiency, as well. Under Napoleon, the French army reached a peak of 200,000 when it prepared for an invasion of Russia. Throughout the 19th century, it was common for armies of 100,000 and more to oppose each other on the battlefield. These armies were largely products of the nations they fought for. The mercenary system had virtually died out in Europe, and the nations could not rely upon volunteers to supply the vast demands upon manpower. There was only one way to obtain the number of men that the new wars demanded: force them to join. This was *conscription*—what is popularly known as the *draft*. This was a far more formal procedure, such as was employed only by modern nations, than the old levies. With it was born the modern mass armies with essentially nonprofessional soldiers performing a soldier's duty for a specified period of time.

Conscription was born during the French Revolution and used with skill by Napoleon to create his gigantic armies. The Prussians, conquered by Napoleon and restricted to a small army, added a twist to conscription. They retained a small body of professionals used to train a large number of civilians, who formed militias. When war came, these militias became full-fledged military units, ready for war.

Conscription was tried by the United States on a limited basis in the Revolutionary War and the War of 1812. The Civil War demanded many more men, however, and conscription was introduced on a larger scale. The Confederacy established conscription in 1862, but the Union used a different approach. In the North, conscription was first tried in the areas that had not produced enough volunteers to meet their quotas. The result was a number of *draft riots* and even armed resistance. The Union leaders solved the problem by recruiting many soldiers and skilled support personnel from northern Europe, promising them "40 acres and a mule" when the war was over.

During the early part of the 19th century, Britain,

France, the United States, and Germany created *war colleges* to train their future officers. Sandhurst and West Point, both started in 1802, were the British and American colleges, respectively. The scientific approach to the development of a body of well-trained men who would have lifelong occupations in the military emerged. Education and training were recognized as vital in furnishing young men with the skills necessary to command modern armies.

The Napoleonic Wars lasted from 1800 to 1815. During that short time, France carved out a huge empire and controlled most of Europe. The principal nations that brought about the collapse of Napoleon were Great Britain and Russia. The British, after the Battle of Trafalgar, controlled the seas, while Napoleon's disastrous invasion of Russia destroyed the French army. Napoleon's final defeat was at Waterloo. There, a combined British, Dutch, and Prussian army beat the French after a fierce battle. This battle pitted the British professional soldier against the conscripted French. The British general, the Duke of Wellington, was outnumbered and took the defensive; the British lines and squares held out against repeated French infantry and cavalry charges, until the Prussian army came onto the field and sealed the fate of the French.

After the Napoleonic Wars, there were no major European conflicts until the Crimean War in the middle of the 19th century. This brutal war pitted the British and French against the Russians. Little can be salvaged from

While women have occasionally disguised themselves as men and enlisted in the army, this Zouave is openly a female soldier. (From Advertising Woodcuts From the Nineteenth-Century Stage, *by Stanley Applebaum, Dover, 1977)*

this conflict except a vague picture of a war caught between the past and the future. It was a mismanaged, bungled operation, ostensibly started to protect the Ottoman Empire from falling into the grasp of the Russians. Thanks to poor supply and gross inefficiency, the French, and especially the British, soldiers suffered dreadfully.

Part of the war witnessed the magnificent British line destroying unwieldy masses of Russian infantry. The British fought as they had during the Napoleonic Wars. At the Battle of Balaclava, a few hundred British troops formed a line to foil a brilliant Russian cavalry maneuver to capture the harbor. These few troops, known as the "thin red line," repulsed the Russian cavalry with a few well-placed volleys. The war also saw the futile Charge of the Light Brigade, during which the British light cavalry, with an almost feudalistic sense of battle, charged the Russian artillery emplacements and was destroyed as an effective unit.

During the Crimean War, disease raged, killing more soldiers than enemy fire. An attempt at instituting a better type of military medical support was undertaken by Florence Nightingale and her staff of *nurses*. Back at home, the British and French people must have thought of the Crimea as some sort of particularly virulent pesthole. Actually, the Crimea was and is widely known as a resort area. But the inefficiencies of supply and medicine had caught up with the large modern armies during this war.

Another war which spanned the past and present was the American Civil War. Although there were plenty of old-fashioned cavalry and bayonet charges, the face of warfare began to change. The soldiers used *rifle muskets*, which fired the mini-ball. The rifle musket provided the infantry with a weapon that could even reach enemy artillery emplacements. In fact, most of the casualties in the Civil War were inflicted by the rifle.

One unusual type of military specialty that was used with great effect during this war was the *sniper*. Both the North and the South had companies of men trained in the use of breech-loading rifles, which were used at ranges considered astonishing in those days. Targets beyond 1,000 yards were attempted with success. Because they used the Sharps rifle, these soldiers were known as *sharpshooters*. On many occasions, snipers killed artillery crews and caused heavy casualties among officers. This specialty has continued and snipers have been present in all wars. However, the Civil War was especially a war of the *rifleman*, so sniping probably was most effective during that conflict. Artillery continued to develop and soon could outrange the best rifle.

Another weapon used during the Civil War gave a taste of what war would be like in the 20th century; this was the Gatling gun. This early version of the *machine gun* was composed of several rifle barrels, which were rotated by a hand crank. With a magazine, this weapon could produce a high rate of fire, which approached that achieved by later automatic weapons.

Armed with modern weapons, the peoples of the East sometimes presented formidable opposition to the supposedly more advanced Western countries. (From **Men: A Pictorial Archive From Nineteenth-Century Sources,** *by Jim Harter, Dover, 1980)*

The breech-loading rifle used by Civil War snipers came into vogue by the time of the Franco-Prussian War in the 1870s. The Prussians used a rifle known as the *needlegun.* The effect of this weapon was remarkable. Soldiers were able to load their weapons from the breech, instead of having to expose themselves as they often did when loading from the muzzle. The breech-loaders also became more accurate and easier to handle than the muzzle-loaders. The rate of fire improved dramatically. With this type of rifle, infantry battles began to change. Lines of soldiers advancing across open fields were too vulnerable. Bayonet attacks became increasingly costly. The objective often became to lure the enemy into attacking a strongly held position, then decimate the attack before launching a counterattack.

By the end of the 19th century, armed forces were still developing at a rapid rate. Powerful new weapons often became obsolete in a matter of decades. For example, the simple single-shot breech-loaders were quickly replaced by magazine-fed, bolt-action rifles. Also, by the end of the century, the use of cavalry was almost over—although a few backward military minds insisted on using cavalry well into the 20th century, as evidenced by the Polish cavalry at the beginning of World War II.

Soldiers were used differently, too. The slow-firing, ponderous lines and columns of troops used at the beginning of the 19th century would have been quickly torn apart by the troops of the last part of the century. To prevent the quick demise of the army, new tactics had to be developed to adapt the infantryman's role to the new battlefield. It was a long, slow process that was not always successful. The infantry through World War I suffered enormous casualties because of modern weapons.

The 20th Century

World War I was thought to be the war to end all wars. It was essentially a political struggle, which engulfed almost all of Europe and involved many countries around the world. The roots of the war were many and complex, ranging from Germany's frustrated colonial ambitions to Britain's fear of German mercantile competition, combined with French antipathy and distrust of Germany. The severity of the war can be directly attributed to the immense destructive force of new weapons, combined with mass national armies.

No one knew what to expect when the war started. Virtually no expert thought that the war would possibly last four years and claim millions of casualties. The French and British were certain that their forces would quickly halt a German thrust and that then they would turn the tables on the kaiser. They also expected a great deal from the huge, ponderous Russian army, which was ready to invade East Prussia. On the other hand, the Germans were confident that they could deal swiftly with the Russians (they did) and simultaneously smash through the Allied forces and win the war in a matter of months. They did not succeed in this regard, although they came very close.

The German army was stalled by the Allies in its attack, and the war degenerated into *trench warfare*, with lines of defensive trenches dug across the French and Belgian countryside. The war became a virtual stalemate. Warfare of this type had never been fought to this degree before. Each side would often take the offensive in a vain effort to break the stalemate. Commanders would order assaults across a stark no-man's-land to try to capture a few yards of ground. Hundreds of thousands of men died in single battles, such as Verdun, Ypres, the Somme, and Gallipoli.

A typical assault would open with a strong artillery barrage, which would attempt to flatten enemy defenses and disrupt enemy concentrations. Then the soldiers would be ordered out of their trenches and on toward the enemy line, across a destroyed, shelled landscape. At this point, enemy artillery and small-arms fire would open up. Holes would begin to appear in the onrushing lines. Machine guns were especially deadly, effectively mowing down advancing troops. There also was a new weapon at hand: *poison gas*. Mustard gas and chlorine gas were used with some limited success by both sides. This only added to the horror of war. If any troops were lucky enough to reach the enemy trenches, they would try to kill the defenders. Then they would prepare for the certain enemy counterattack, aimed at retaking any lost territory.

The soldiers who fought through this dirty, soul-breaking type of warfare were, overwhelmingly, conscripted troops. They suffered through long periods of debilitating disease in the trenches and shorter moments of terror as they attacked or were attacked. The higher command never seemed to be able to figure a way out of the bloody stalemate and simply tried to throw more men at the enemy in an effort to win. This form of warfare proved to be a great consumer of men and equipment.

This new type of warfare had a far-reaching effect on military organization. The French and Germans had conscription plans well in effect. The British, following long-standing traditions, resisted the use of conscription for much of the war. First, they relied upon a small

In the 20th century, modern warfare has changed the face of the East, here in China, as well as the West. (From The New America and the Far East, *by G. Waldo Browne, 1901)*

professional army, but it was soon destroyed. Then the British turned to volunteers. They were successful until 1916, when they were forced by the enormous scope of the war to conscript civilians for the army. Millions of troops were used in the war. The total number that was mobilized by all the participants mounted to over 65,000,000 men. The ultimate cost in lives was enormous, too. Battle deaths alone mounted to over 8,000,000, and more than 20,000,000 were wounded.

To convince their people that their cause was right, the governments of the various countries used another form of warfare—both against the enemy and on their own populations. This was *propaganda*. Enemy atrocities were detailed and exaggerated, while the noble nature of their own soldiers was extolled. In the meantime, propaganda was used in an attempt to undercut the morale of enemy troops by convincing them that they had no chance of winning.

The period between World War I and World War II began well. The *League of Nations* was established, and an era of prosperity helped the world get back on its feet. Millions of demobilized soldiers returned to civilian life, as nations began to disarm. There was an attempt to police the less-developed regions of the Earth. But the League failed. The era of prosperity suddenly vanished, and totalitarian regimes sprang up around the world. The most important of these totalitarian countries were Germany, Italy, Japan, and the Soviet Union. All of these countries were interested in expanding their spheres of influence. Ultimately, they helped plunge the world once again into a global conflict.

Invention and scientific progress continued after World War I ended. The flimsy aircraft of World War I developed into massive, sophisticated engines of destruction. Slow, cumbersome *tanks* evolved into swift, powerful, almost unstoppable machines. Then the scientific genius for destruction came up with a brand new weapon, the *missile*, a link with the nuclear age.

New advances in science were easily transferred to the military. Electricity and the internal combustion engine, the airplane and radio, later electronics and computer science were adopted by the military, a process that has continued with today's "smart" weapons, which have their own internal guidance systems. New twists, such as *sonar* and *radar*, were added.

Whole industries sprang up to supply the military. *Scientists, technologists, manufacturers, contractors* all vied—and still vie—with one another to sell their products to the armed forces. During the late 19th century, rifled cannon were hawked by Krupp, the giant German arms manufacturer. Today, many American companies try to sell fighter planes and compete with other manufacturers for lucrative government contracts.

The basic occupational groups in the military remained the same. The infantry was given much more efficient weapons—*bazookas*, automatic rifles, better machine guns, submachine guns, more powerful grenades, better mortars. The task of the infantryman was much the same, although there was more of a trend toward specialization. The new army became more mechanized, with animals being almost totally replaced by trucks and jeeps. However, the mechanized army required more support than ever before. A host of troops were *cooks, clerks, mechanics, military police, medics, quartermasters*, and the like.

In a number of ways, World War II was similar to World War I. During the initial stage of the war, it was essentially Britain and France fighting Nazi Germany. As in the first war, Germany quickly gained the upper hand. By 1940, the Germans controlled most of Europe. Applying principles learned during the Spanish Civil War, they defeated Allied armies with lightning *panzer* (armored) thrusts, in combination with pinpoint dive-bombing followed by swift infantry support. As France was about to fall to the German armies in June 1940, the British army was barely rescued at Dunkirk. Germany prepared to invade the British Isles and stepped up both surface and submarine attacks on British shipping.

But the British had a combination of skill and luck working in their favor. Their air force was unmatched in fighter planes and pilots, and they had a technological advantage in the form of radar. Radar gave the British a tremendous edge by indicating when and where the German air attacks would appear.

Another type of warfare that was much improved during World War II was *espionage*. Here the Allies had the upper hand. The British possessed a decoding machine, which enabled them to break German messages.

Propaganda and political sabotage were also improved. In keeping with the total war concept, every attempt was made to undermine the opposing government in any way. The idea of a *fifth column* grew up. This term was coined during the Spanish Civil War, when General Quepio de Llano, a rebel commander, approached Madrid with four columns of troops. He described his supporters in the city as a "fifth column."

Modern soldiers have had to shift their sights to meet threats from the skies. (National Archives, Records of the United States Coast Guard, 26-G-2477, c. 1943)

This phrase has become synonymous with treason and subversion from within.

The Germans were particularly successful with this type of warfare, which helped cause the collapse of Hungary and Czechoslovakia. They were also masters at discovering puppets to head their conquered territories. In France, they used Marshal Pétain, a respected World War I figure. In Norway, they used Quisling, a man whose name became a common noun meaning *traitor*.

As World War II was another modern, total war, it demanded huge numbers of troops. The total mobilized by all participating countries was more than 100,000,000. Total military dead was more than 15,000,000, and civilian dead amounted to more than 30,000,000.

Other developments in World War II would affect modern warfare. The Germans invented the *jet fighter*, too late to be of any use in World War II, but with potential for the future. Aircraft, in fact, became a very important military arm. The United States carrier forces were indispensable in the defeat of the strong Japanese fleet in the Pacific.

But to sum up World War II, one must look at the end of the war. The *atomic bomb*, dropped on Nagasaki and Hiroshima, became the symbol of war to come. Wedded to the German missile technology, the nuclear bomb has become the ultimate weapon.

To a major degree, the modern world is a result of World War II. The East, dominated by the Soviet Union, and the West, dominated by the United States, have maintained hostilities of varying degrees since the end of the war. The two superpowers have often fought through the use of surrogates. The Korean and Vietnam wars are examples of these types of local surrogate wars.

The hostility between the major powers has contributed to the development of an amazing number of sophisticated weapons. Modern warfare is totally mechanized and is approaching a high degree of automation, thanks to new *computer* technology. Even outer space is seen as a potential battlefield, with killer *satellites* and orbital *missile stations* within the realm of

At Arlington Cemetery on Memorial Day, 1941, this soldier's face speaks of sadness for those who have died and of deaths soon to come. (By Esther Bubley, Library of Congress)

possibility. In response, the military has need of a number of specialized occupations found in civilian businesses: *computer operators, programmers, systems engineers, computer engineers, mechanics, pilots, chemists, biologists, doctors,* and many others.

The traditional occupations have changed somewhat in concept, but are still recognizable. A squad of infantry now may carry the destructive power of an entire World War II brigade. Hand-held missiles, new types of rocket-propelled grenades, defensive mines, all combine to give the infantry soldier even more strength in the field. A variety of "smart" weapons are used. These technical marvels are rapidly becoming easier to use. The only difficulty is that they are hard to repair under combat conditions, so the infantryman may ultimately be forced to rely upon trusted small arms.

Soldiers are also now trained to face different types of modern assaults. These can be conventional or they may be nuclear, chemical, or even biological. Although supposedly used in only a few minor engagements since World War I, poisonous gas, especially in the form of nerve gas, has been greatly improved. Major countries still have stockpiles of deadly viruses and chemicals with which to attack population centers and food and water sources.

The field of espionage has been enhanced by new computer and electronic advances. Huge mainframe computers analyze masses of data about the enemy, while satellites, spy planes, microwave equipment, and all sorts of bugging devices keep track of potential enemies. Weapons of assassination have been improved, although the skill of the agents may be little different. These weapons range from remote-controlled bombs to virtually microscopic pellets containing highly toxic poison.

One type of activity on the increase is *terrorism*. Causes run the gamut of political thought. They include the Irish Republican Army, the Palestine Liberation Organization, the Red Brigade, and numerous others. In some cases, the organizations are fronts for major powers. In other cases, they are home-grown groups attempting to overthrow what they perceive is a bad government or to influence international affairs in their favor. Although they have existed from the earliest times, *resistance fighters* are particularly well suited to today's social environment.

Mercenaries, too, are still active, primarily in Third World countries. The rise of national armies substantially reduced the dependence upon mercenaries in world affairs, but trained mercenaries are always in demand. For example, in World War II, Claire L. Chennault created a mercenary organization known as the Flying Tigers. This group of American soldiers fought for the Chinese government against the Japanese before the United States entered the war.

More recently, mercenaries have played important roles in the countless African struggles. Small groups of soldiers, primarily Europeans, were paid to strengthen many African armies in places like Biafra, the Congo, Rhodesia, and South Africa. These mercenaries brought Western skills and technology to the African jungles and veldts. They spanned the range of modern *soldiers of fortune*—commanders, infantry, armorers, pilots, weapons experts, and support people. Central and South American countries also use their share of mercenaries. Many American "advisors" have been hired to supervise the security services and armed forces of countries in that area of the world. Oil-rich Arab countries, too—like the rich kingdoms of thousands of years ago—prefer to buy their warriors instead of trusting their own people.

Mercenaries have often been among the foremost in keeping up to date with military hardware. They were among the first to adopt firearms, and the best gunners also were soldiers of fortune. To this day, mercenaries try to stay in the forefront of new developments. It is highly doubtful that mercenaries will ever disappear from combat. The world has plenty of highly trained warriors looking for employment.

Other changes have taken place in the modern military, too. Where once officers were drawn from the highest social classes in some countries, such as Britain and Prussia, officers are increasingly drawn from the middle classes. Training, desire, and ability have become more important than social class. Many minorities and women can now become officers, as well as join the ranks. In the process, military officers have, as a class, lost something of their former status. Even as late as the 1950s, a United States President, Dwight D. Eisenhower, was a former general. But many lower-ranking military officers in North America and Europe today have less status than schoolteachers. On the other hand, in communist countries, where military leaders are deliberately drawn from among the proletariat (working class), status is as high as it ever was. And in many countries around the world, notably in South America and Africa, but also in Eurasia, the military has simply taken over the political leadership of the country.

Warfare has come a long way from the days when people first gathered together to fight one another. Soldiers today have weapons of enormous power, which can be launched by the push of a button or the pull of a trigger. The days when a soldier's effectiveness depended upon strength and personal prowess are, if not totally ended, much diminished.

The modern military has, in many countries, become an employer like any other industry. In the United States, massive advertising campaigns try to lure young men—and increasingly women—into the armed services. The advertising sells them upon the idea that the military is where they can gain experience that will serve them in good stead when they search for employment in civilian life.

And, like any modern industry, the military has needs for a wide variety of skilled and semiskilled workers to keep the organization going. Desk jobs are just as much in evidence, if not more so, as actual combat occupations. This is necessary because the modern military is a highly complex organization that exists year in, year out. Supply, records processing, salary, benefits procurement, all place their demands upon the operation. It is a far cry from the days when a king would demand his vassals to gather together for a limited amount of time.

Yet for all the change, the object remains the same. Whether soldiers are armed with a spear, *francisca*, machine gun, Spitfire, or ICBM, they fight to destroy the enemy, using whatever means are available. And there

In modern times, numerous soldiers serve almost purely ceremonial functions. (By Gustave Doré, from London: A Pilgrimage, 1872)

has not been that much change in tactics. Modern commanders are likely to study the ancient battles of Greece and Rome to obtain insight into warfare. Feints, flank attacks, and probes for weaknesses may now be on a global scale, but they have the same objective today as 2,000 years ago.

For related occupations in this volume, *Warriors and Adventurers*, see the following:
    Flyers
    Robbers and Other Criminals
    Sailors
    Spies

For related occupations in other volumes of the series, see the following:
in *Builders*:
    Architects and Contractors
    Construction Laborers
    Roadbuilders
    Shipwrights
    Tunnelers

in *Communicators*:
    Clerks
    Messengers and Couriers
in *Financiers and Traders*:
    Merchants and Shopkeepers
in *Harvesters*:
    Hunters
in *Healers* (forthcoming):
    Nurses
    Physicians and Surgeons
in *Helpers and Aides*:
    Drivers
    Private Guards and Detectives
in *Leaders and Lawyers*:
    Police Officers
    Political Leaders
    Prison Guards and Executioners
    Secret Police
in *Manufacturers and Miners* (forthcoming):
    Factory Workers
    Mechanics and Repairers
    Metalsmiths
    Weapon Makers
in *Performers and Players* (forthcoming):
    Athletes
in *Restaurateurs and Innkeepers* (forthcoming):
    Cooks
in *Scientists and Technologists*:
    Alchemists
    Biologists
    Chemists
    Computer Scientists
    Engineers
    Mathematicians
    Physicists

Spies

The occupation of *spy* is hazily defined. Throughout the ages, the most successful spies have been those who have kept their identities secret. Perhaps the best description is that spies are like chameleons; they blend into the surroundings they are investigating. In order to accomplish their tasks, spies—or *counterspies*—make use of a wide variety of skills to keep themselves hidden from public view. Spying has always been surrounded by mystery. Few spies are made public figures—unless, of course, they are unsuccessful and are caught.

The objectives of espionage are simple. One side attempts to gather information about another, generally a competitor or potential competitor. The other side tries to prevent this. It is a dangerous game that has been played for thousands of years.

For as long as we know, armies have employed some

sort of information-gathering arm. An early king or chief desiring military or economic information about a rival probably engaged the first spy—or perhaps he acted as a spy himself, as would occasionally happen throughout history. Legend has it, for example, that in the ninth century, King Alfred the Great of England disguised himself as a *minstrel* in order to gather military information from an invading Viking force.

While much spying throughout history has consisted of gathering information from direct observation, people and institutions very early began to develop codes—and *code breakers*. When writing was first being developed, it was itself a code, for so few people could read. But as literacy spread, most of the ancient peoples—in Egypt, Mesopotamia, China, and India—developed some sort of simple code to keep their messages from the prying eyes of spies. The Greeks, especially the Spartans, made use of *cryptography* and even wrote about using the encoding process to protect their own communications, while continuing to use spies for observation and *double agents* for misleading the enemy. The Moslems developed a wide range of secret codes; more important, they developed a scientific approach to analyzing codes, producing probably the first true *cryptographers* or *cryptanalysts*. But, as far as we know, their approach did not spread and in time degenerated in their own world.

With the increase in military, diplomatic, religious, and business correspondence in Renaissance Europe, cryptography took on a new life. Because communications were routinely opened and read by spies representing various institutions, correspondents began to develop codes. In response, some groups—notably in Italy, both among the Papal States and the commercial city-states—adopted the procedure of opening important documents, copying their contents, resealing them, and sending them on to "black chambers," where cryptanalysts set about working to decode them. In the process, both cryptography and cryptanalysis became increasingly more sophisticated. By the 18th century, Leon Battista Alberti, often called the father of Western cryptography, was writing books on the subject, and recommending the use of a *cipher disk*, a wheel that can be set up to help people decode messages. The development and breaking of codes became increasingly important during the years of the religious wars, when Catholics and Protestants battled for control of Europe, and in the subsequent era of political upheaval foreshadowing the rise of modern democracies.

Meanwhile, spying of the more direct sort continued unabated. No less a person than Daniel Defoe, author of *Robinson Crusoe*, worked as an effective agent for the English. He worked tirelessly to expose plots and undermined several promising schemes that threatened the Hanoverian crown.

As a strict occupation, spying has always been a part-time job for the vast majority of those engaged. These

The penalty for spying is often death; here Nathan Hale is to die for his country. (By Felix O.C. Darley, 1776, from The American Revolution: A Picture Sourcebook, *by John Grafton, Dover, 1975)*

part-time spies were ordinary people, generally serving as the eyes and ears of a *spymaster*—an individual spreading and gathering an espionage net in hope of catching some vital information. Though some have become spies out of patriotic motives, many others have simply taken to spying for the money they might make selling information. *Innkeepers, bartenders*, and *maids*

The spying possibilities of ballooning are caricatured in this mid-19th-century cartoon. ("Modern Balooning," by George Cruikshank, 1851)

were among those commonly chosen as spies. More recently, *reporters* and traveling *scientists* have been used. Indeed, many countries engaged the services of their *diplomats* to gather information in the host countries. The Soviet Union has long engaged spies from their intelligence organization, the KGB, as members of embassies. And when the Iranians seized the United States Embassy in Teheran, they claimed to have captured people and documents of the Central Intelligence Agency (CIA).

One occupation that has often had quite an impact on spying is prostitution. *Call girls* are often well placed to gather particularly sensitive information. In the 1960s, the British government was rocked by scandal when it was discovered that a prominent cabinet member was having an affair with a call girl, Christine Keeler, who was also a companion of a Russian naval attaché. The attaché had used Keeler in an effort to discover information about the delivery of some nuclear weapons in Germany.

The means of obtaining sensitive material have often been convoluted and shady. The weaknesses of others have always been exploited. Bribery and blackmail are two of the spy's major weapons. Many unsuspecting people over the centuries have fallen into the grasp of some spy looking for information. This was the spy of literature—the intrepid explorer penetrating the heart of enemy country and engaging in all sorts of daring exploits. Most often, however, the spy's work has been the routine gathering of information, punctuated by brief times of extreme danger. Today the vast majority of occupations in espionage are even more mundane, for the computer age has taken over.

The modern superspy is a *technologist*. To gather and sift through information of great variety and volume, the modern spy uses a fantastic array of electronic surveillance equipment. Satellites, microwave equipment, and telephone monitoring devices are all in use, gathering raw information. The Soviet Union's KGB, the

United States' CIA, and similar organizations are all collecting an enormous mass of data.

The real trick, however, is not the gathering, but the interpreting. This is where massive banks of computers are used. They sort and categorize the raw data. Of course, people still have to make sense of all this information, employing all their skills and experience in a fantastically involved and complicated operation.

The work can be reduced sometimes if the spy can read sensitive material of the enemy—secret material which is sent in coded form. The greatest coup for any intelligence organization is still breaking the enemy's code. This lets the spies know exactly what the opposition is planning. The British, for example, obtained a copy of the German code machine, called *Enigma*, just before the start of World War II. A Pole who had worked on the German machine built a mock-up of the machine for British Intelligence. The British decided they needed an actual machine, so with help from the Polish Secret Service, they got one. Then British *cryptographers* got to work and discovered the German code.

Throughout World War II, the British were able to read German messages and transmissions. They knew beforehand of almost every major German operation. This, of course, was a very powerful weapon—and one which had to be jealously guarded, so the Germans could never figure out that the code had been broken. To this end, Churchill sacrificed the city of Coventry to a major air raid, rather than expose the Enigma secret.

Few things are straightforward in electronic espionage, however; there still is the human factor. The United States had broken the Japanese code before America entered the war, but the Americans were still caught by surprise at Pearl Harbor because they did not react fast enough to the information they had.

For all the electronic methods of obtaining information, a dedicated *intelligence agent* is still important. Occasionally, newspaper accounts hint at some major espionage case. For example, in 1982, it was revealed that a British employee at a super-secret electronic communications center had been actually feeding important information about British and American code breaking to the Russians throughout the 1970s. However, in the twisted world of spying, all is not necessarily what the papers uncover. Was this agent truly in the pay of the Russians, was he a dupe of the British, or was he a double or even triple agent? In all probability the total truth will never be known.

There is another, even darker side to espionage—*sabotage*. This involves using a wide variety of activities, from rumors to violent force, in attempts to undermine an opponent's ability to function effectively. The term *fifth column* originated during the Spanish Civil War when the rebel leader, General Quepio de Llano, claimed to have four columns of soldiers converging on Madrid and a fifth column of *subversives* ready to strike within the city. Of course, the fifth column was nothing new. *Traitors* have appeared throughout history, but modern technology is providing subversives with the means to be ever more effective. In recent years,

The Civil War often divided family members; here Confederate spy Belle Lamar is in the custody of her husband, a Union leader. (Advertising woodcut from Belle Lamar, *New York, 1874)*

assassinations, violent overthrow of governments, and destruction of industries have become commonplace. Countries such as Libya and the Soviet Union have actively supported international *terrorism*, which is a form of espionage. And the United States has been known to replace governments it did not approve of by sponsoring coups and revolutions. This form of espionage is directed at all segments of the population—government, industry, the entire populace. Its aim is to sow confusion, to weaken the country, perhaps to encourage revolution.

To counter terrorism, many countries have developed special units, either in the police or the armed forces. For example, Britain's SAS (Special Air Service) and SBS (Special Boat Squadron) were formed to deal with all types of terrorist acts, such as foiling the seizure of embassies. They have also been very active in Northern Ireland, fighting the Irish Republican Army (IRA) undercover. The SBS, which was active as an advanced reconnaissance unit in the Falkland Islands War, has a peacetime duty of protecting the North Sea oil fields from seizure or terrorism.

In the Middle East, terrorism is almost a way of life. Assassinations are common. The word *assassination* itself, as we have seen, comes from a group of religious-political fanatics who used murder as a weapon to control Iran and the surrounding territory for some centuries, until the Mongols exterminated the terrorists—but not their ideas—in the late 13th century.

Today, espionage is a combination of the classic spy approach and the computerized search for information. The world is in the midst of an information age. Almost everything worth knowing is digitized and stored in the memory banks of computers. Technology has provided the means to pry into almost every corner of the earth. The Americans and the Soviets have satellites which can scan the world and relay all the data they gather back to computers for interpretation.

Espionage occupations, therefore, are overwhelmingly technical today. Many spies have traded in their trenchcoats for white lab coats. Yet always lurking out in the cold are the few professionals we seldom hear about. These men and women continue to spread their nets in the same old way, living a secret, dangerous life to get the most vital information.

For related occupations in this volume, *Warriors and Adventurers*, see the following:
  Flyers
  Robbers and Other Criminals
  Sailors
  Soldiers

For related occupations in other volumes of the series, see the following:
in *Communicators*:
  Authors
  Journalists and Broadcasters
  Messengers and Couriers
in *Helpers and Aides*:
  Servants and Other Domestic Laborers
in *Leaders and Lawyers*:
  Diplomats
  Political Leaders
  Prison Guards and Executioners
  Secret Police
in *Performers and Players* (forthcoming):
  Musicians
in *Restaurateurs and Innkeepers* (forthcoming):
  Innkeepers
  Prostitutes
in *Scholars and Priests* (forthcoming):
  Priests
in *Scientists and Technologists* (forthcoming):
  Chemists
  Computer Scientists
  Engineers
  Physicists

Suggestions for Further Reading

For further information about the occupations in this family, you may wish to consult the books below.

General

Canby, Courtlandt. *A History of Weaponry*. New York: Hawthorne Books, 1963. An illustrated look at the evolution of warfare.

Dupuy, R. Ernest, and Trevor N. Dupuy. *The Encyclopedia of Military History from 3500 B.C. to the Present*, rev. ed. New York: Harper and Row, 1977. A magnificent, exhaustive work giving an overview of military actions around the world at all times in history.

Dupuy, T.N. *The Evolution of Weapons and Warfare.* Indianapolis: Bobbs-Merrill, 1980. An excellent companion work; an intelligent discussion of the development of warfare.

Elliot, J.H. *Imperial Spain 1469-1716.* New York: Mentor, 1963. Focuses on Spain during the period of its military dominance in Europe.

Fitzgerald, C.P. *China: A Short Cultural History.* Taiwan: Book World, 1961. Contains material about this country's unique approach to warfare.

Kluckhohn, Clyde, and Dorothea Leighton. *The Navaho.* New York: Doubleday Anchor, 1962. Includes material on tribal warfare.

MacManus, Seumas. *The Story of the Irish Race.* New York: Devin-Adair, 1970. Includes good material on military topics throughout the history of Ireland.

McCartney, Eugene S. *Warfare by Land and Sea.* New York: Cooper Square Publishers, 1963. A good general history.

Oakeshott, R.E. *The Archaeology of Weapons.* New York: Praeger, 1960. A good description of the development of killing tools.

Payne-Gallway, Sir Ralph. *The Crossbow: Mediaeval and Modern Military and Sporting: Its Construction, History and Management.* New York: Bramhall, 1963. An excellent, detailed work about the most feared medieval weapon.

Stone, George Cameron. *A Glossary of the Construction, Decoration and Use of Arms and Armor in All Countries and in All Times.* New York: Jack Brussel Publisher, 1934. A fine sourcebook that describes virtually every imaginable weapon; particularly good for Asian weapons.

Sulzberger, C.L. *The American Heritage Picture History of World War II*. New York: American Heritage, 1966. A popular, illustrated treatment of World War II.

Wedgwood, C.V. *The Thirty Years War*. New York: Anchor, 1961. One of the best histories of this devastating series of wars.

Flyers

Kelly, Charles J., Jr. *The Sky's the Limit: The History of the Airlines*. New York: Coward-McCann, 1963. On planes and pilots, an especially effective description of the industry's pioneers.

Gamblers and Gamesters

Fleming, Alice. *Something for Nothing: A History of Gambling*. New York: Delacorte, 1978. A colorful description of gambling and professional gamblers throughout history.

Robbers and Other Criminals

Abbot, Daniel J. *Crime in Developing Countries: A Comparative Perspective*. New York: Wiley, 1973. On modern criminality in the Third World; particularly good for Uganda and India.

Auboyer, Jeannine. *Daily Life in Ancient India, 200 B.C.-700 A.D*. New York: Macmillan, 1968. Contains good information about the treatment of criminals in ancient Indian society.

Chalidze, Valery. *Criminal Russia*. New York: Random House, 1977. Good on historical Russian crime, its social impact and organization; somewhat sketchy on present-day criminal activity, relying much on hearsay.

Chevalier, Louis. *Laboring Classes and Dangerous Classes in Paris during the First Half of the Nineteenth Century.* New York: Howard Fertig, 1973. Translated by Frank Jellinek. Details the tremendous amount of crime and its social impact during the period.

Inciaro, James A. *Careers in Crime.* Chicago: Rand McNally, 1975. A very informative, readable survey of professional criminal occupations in the history of Western society.

Maurer, David W. *The American Confidence Man.* Springfield, Ill.: Charles C. Thomas, 1974. Includes much detail on the history, personalities, methods, and social status of grifters.

Montet, Pierre. *Everyday Life in Ancient Egypt in the Days of Ramses the Great.* London: Edward Arnold, 1962. Especially good for descriptions of organized temple and grave robbing.

Tobias, J. *Crime and Industrial Society in the 19th Century.* New York: Schocken, 1967. Tremendously detailed, particularly about industrial England and the almost infinite gradations of professional crime.

Weisser, Michael K. *Crime and Punishment in Early Modern Europe.* Sussex, Eng.: Harvester Press, 1979. Useful for the development of medieval crime, particularly in England but also on the Continent.

Sailors

American Pilots' Association. *State Pilotage in America: Historical Outline with European Background.* Washington, D.C.: American Pilots' Association, 1979. A fascinating book, written for the trade.

Gruppe, Henry E., and the Editors of Time-Life Books. *The Frigates*. Alexandria, Virginia: Time-Life Books, 1979. A beautifully illustrated book.

Haws, Duncan. *Ships and the Sea: A Chronological Review*. New York: Thomas Y. Crowell, 1975. On the evolution of ships.

The History of the Sailing Ship. New York: Arco Publishing Company, 1975. A nice treatment of the development of the masted ship.

Johnson, Captain Charles. *A General History of the Robberies and Murders of the Most Notorious Pirates*. London: Routledge and Kegan Paul, 1926. Arthur L. Hayward, ed. A colorful look at pirates and buccaneers.

Kemp, Lieutenant Commander Peter, ed. *Encylopedia of Ships and Seafaring*. New York: Crown, 1980.

————, ed. *The History of the Royal Navy*. New York: Putnam, 1969. A fine treatment of the world's most successful navy.

Lloyd, Christopher. *The British Seaman: 1200-1860: A Social Survey*. Rutherford, New Jersey: Fairleigh Dickenson University Press, 1968. Provides an excellent portrayal of the men who became British sailors, and how they were treated at different periods of history.

Macintyre, Donald. *Sea Power in the Pacific: A History from the Sixteenth Century to the Present Day*. New York: Crane, Russak, 1972. A good historical work, concentrating on the shifting balance of sea power in the Pacific.

Mahan, Alfred Thayer. *The Influence of Sea Power upon History 1660-1805*. Englewood Cliffs, New Jersey: Prentice-Hall, 1980.

Marcus, G.J. *Heart of Oak: A Survey of British Sea Power in the Georgian Era*. London: Oxford University Press, 1975. An excellent portrait of the British sailor over the centuries.

Martin, Paul. *European Military Uniforms: A Short History*. London: Spring Books, 1967. A brief look at the evolution of uniforms.

Mordal, Jacques. *Twenty-five Centuries of Sea Warfare*. New York: Clarkson N. Potter, 1959. Translated by Len Ortzen. On all eras of naval warfare.

Rodgers, William Ledyard. *Greek and Roman Naval Warfare: A Study of Strategy, Tactics, and Ship Design from Salamis (480 B.C.) to Actium (31 B.C.)*. Annapolis, Maryland: United States Naval Institute, 1937. An important discussion of ancient naval warfare and some battles that changed the course of history.

————. *Naval Warfare Under Oars, 4th to 16th Centuries: A Study of Strategy, Tactics and Ship Design*. Annapolis, Maryland: United States Naval Institute, 1940. On galley warfare.

Soldiers

Aston, Trevor, ed. *Crisis in Europe 1560-1660*. New York: Anchor, 1967. A series of articles about one of Europe's most tumultuous periods; includes an especially good article about mercenaries.

Bennett, H.S. *Life on the English Manor*. Cambridge: At the University Press, 1969. A close look at the social organization of a feudal manor; includes material on military service.

Blair, Peter Hunter. *An Introduction to Anglo-Saxon England*. Cambridge: At the University Press, 1966. A well-researched work, including material on Anglo-Saxon and Viking soldiers.

Dickson, Paul. *The Electronic Battlefield*. Bloomington: Indiana University Press, 1976. On modern warfare.

Duffy, Christopher. *Fire and Stone: The Science of Fortress Warfare 1660-1860*. Newton Abbot, London: David and Charles, 1975. Has a useful focus on the development of fortresses and siegecraft.

Ellis, John. *Cavalry: The History of Mounted Warfare*. New York: Putnam, 1978. On the development of the horse soldier.

————. *The Social History of the Machine Gun*. New York: Pantheon Books, 1975. Has an interesting focus on a weapon that changed the face of the modern battlefield.

Ganshof, F.L. *Feudalism*. New York: Harper, 1961. An excellent, important work that deals with the evolution of feudalism.

Goode, Stephen. *Guerilla Warfare and Terrorism*. New York: Franklin Watts, 1977. A good treatment of nontraditional warfare, with a focus on this century.

Peterson, Harold L. *Round Shot and Rammers*. New York: Bonanza, 1969. On artillery.

Protz, William B., Jr. *Wargamer's Guide to the English Civil War*. Milwaukee, Wisconsin: Z & M Enterprises, 1974. An interesting look at Cromwell's Roundheads and Charles's Cavaliers from a wargamer's perspective; good on arms and tactics.

Robinson, H. Russell, F.S.A. *Oriental Armour*. New York: Walker, 1967. A fine work that concentrates on Asian armor.

The R.O.T.C. Manual. Engineers, Basic., 2nd ed. Washington, D.C.: National Service Publishing Company, 1931. Training manual for the post-World War I soldier.

Tactics and Techniques of Infantry, Advanced. Washington, D.C.: The National Service Publishing Company, 1931. Another "how to" book for American infantry, covering weapons, tactics, and specific battles.

Watson, G.R. *The Roman Soldier.* Ithaca, New York: Cornell University Press, 1969. A fine, well-researched treatment of the Roman soldier in the Republic and Empire; covers the evolution of tactics, arms, and formations.

Spies

Haldane, R.A. *The Hidden World.* New York: St. Martin's, 1976. On the world of cryptography and the people working in it.

Haswell, Jock. *Spies and Spymasters: A Concise History of Intelligence.* London: Thames and Hudson, 1977. A brief illustrated work, focusing on the modern period.

Orlov, Alexander. *Handbook of Intelligence and Guerrilla Warfare.* Ann Arbor: University of Michigan Press, 1972. Spying from the perspective of a Soviet intelligence officer.

Winterbotham, F.W. *The Ultra Secret.* New York: Harper & Row, 1974. An interesting account of how Britain broke Germany's code in World War II.

Index